GW00728970

BOBBING
Two Thousand Years of
Kentish History

First published 2007 by:

Mifair Publishing – Potters Bar, Herts, England

ISBN 978-0-9543967-1-8

Typeset in 11pt Times
Drawings by Peter Judges and Michael Fairley
Design by Concept Design
Printed in England by Jameson Press, Hertfordshire

Michael Fairley

Peter Judges and Dorothy Fairley

BOBBING
Two Thousand Years of Kentish History

Dedication

This book is dedicated to my mother, Dorothy Fairley, without whose years of initial research and notes on the history of Bobbing this book would never have been written.

Through these pages her memory will live on.

Michael Fairley

Contents

Front cover illustrations:

Centre – detail from a map of 1769 showing Bobbing Court.

Clockwise from top right – Sir Arnold Savage of Bobbing Court in Lancastrian armour in 1410, Bobbing church 2007, Gore Court Cricket ground in the 1960s, Mackelden farm workers in the 1930s, Catherine Clifford of Bobbing Court (circa 1562) and stained glass window in Bobbing Church.

Preface

I am delighted to be able to commend this excellent history of one of the lesser-known villages of the Swale Borough. It is very easy to pass Bobbing without noticing that it is there. It can not be seen from the new A249 to Sheppey and the A2 just skirts one boundary. The village appears not to have a natural centre and there is no historical house or building to attract the attention of a casual visitor. In spite of that, the people who have lived there over the centuries have contributed to our country and to our county in significant ways.

The beauty of this book is that it clearly sets the story of the village in the context of the flow of history. The macrocosm of our nation can be seen in the microcosm of this village. The effects of national movements, disasters and changes can be seen in the lives of the residents in this parish.

We seem to be living in an age when more and more research is being done into individual localities as well as in genealogical studies. The Internet has put at our disposal a wealth of records which have been underused and the result is the blossoming of local histories. In this corner of Kent we have seen the publication of collections of old photographs of Sittingbourne. We have an excellent history of the village of Borden and booklets have appeared on Bredgar and Upchurch. Now it is the turn of Bobbing and Michael Fairley, with the help of Peter Judges and initial research carried out by Michael's mother in the 1950s and 1960s, has made an excellent job of it.

I commend this book on the history of Bobbing to all who have an interest in the local history of the villages of Kent.

Peter J Morgan

Chairman of Sittingbourne Heritage Museum

History timeline for Bobbing

Evidence of farming settlements dating back to the Stone Age — *from 2,300 BC*

Settlement by followers of Bobba — *before 150 BC*

Occupation by Romans and building of Watling Street — *from 43 AD*

Romans withdraw from England — *401 AD*

Jutish chieftans Hengist and Horsa arrive to defend - and then control - Kent. — *440 AD*

Bobbing becomes part of Royal Jutish Estate. Oisc, son of Hengist, first Saxon King of Kent — *488 AD*

St Augustine welcomed to Kent by King Ethelbert, converts county to Christianity — *560 AD*

Augustine becomes first Archbishop of Canterbury — *597 AD*

Missionary foundation established in Bobbing by Sexburga, prioress of Minster Priory — *670 AD*

Danes begin raids into Kent and lay waste to great areas of county. Milton plundered — *835-897 AD*

King Alfred gathers army at Bayford Castle, Milton, to resist Danes — *897 AD*

Danes again invade and take over British
throne under King Canute   *1016 AD*

England remains under Saxon rule until
Battle of Hastings   *1066 AD*

Odo of Bayeaux becomes largest landowner
in Kent   *1067 AD*

Ralph de Savage living at Bobbing Court   *1187 AD*

King Stephen and King John regularly visit
Norwood Castle, Bobbing, to hunt
in forest   *1100-1200 AD*

Land in Bobbing owned by Minster Priory   *1186 AD*

Ralph de Savage with Richard I
at Siege of Acon   *1190-94 AD*

Bobbing Church built   *before 1230 AD*

Bobbing Church and tithes given
to Minster Priory by Henry III   *1234 AD*

Sir Thomas de Savage and Sir Roger de Savage
of Bobbing with King Edward at Siege
of Caerlaverock   *1300AD*

Black death sweeps across Kent. 45% of
population die   *1348 AD*

Watt Tyler rebellion joined by local men. March
along Watling Street   *1381 AD*

Sir Arnold Savage of Bobbing twice speaker
of House of Commons and High Sheriff
of Kent   *1385 AD*

Eleanor Savage of Bobbing Court marries
Sir William de Clifford   *1405 AD*

Cade rebellion joined by local men   *1450 AD*

Nicholas de Clifford of Bobbing knighted by
Earl of Essex at Rouen   *1591 AD*

First cherry orchards planted in Bobbing   *1590s*

Sir Nicholas Clifford sails in Amada with
Sir John Hawkins and Sir Francis Drake to
fight Spanish. Mortally shot in battle   *1595 AD*

Sir Conyers Clifford of Bobbing becomes Privy
Councellor of Ireland. Sent to relieve besieged
Calooney Castle. Ambushed and killed   *1599 AD*

Thomas Greene of Bobbing sails to new colonies.
Becomes Provincial Governor of Maryland   *1647 AD*

Great Plague devastates London and Kent.
Thousands die   *1666-67 AD*

Titus Oates preferred to the vicarage
of Bobbing   *1673 AD*

Flour mill established at Bobbing Hill before 1760 AD

Swing Riots by poor farm labourers come to Bobbing	*1830 AD*
London, Chatham, Dover Railway built through Bobbing	*1858 AD*
Waterworks established at Keycol Hill	*1868 AD*
Severe weather damages orchards. Ice flows in Thames	*1867-95 AD*
Bobbing Church of England School built	*1869 AD*
Bobbing Oak planted for Queen Victoria's Jubilee	*1887 AD*
Bobbing Parish Council established	*1895 AD*
First traffic lights in Kent installed at Key Street	*1937 AD*
Messerschmitt shot down and crashes behind Bobbing School	*1940 AD*
German VI rocket fell in Bobbing	*1944 AD*
Foundation stone laid for Bobbing Village Hall	*1953 AD*
Multi-level road interchange and new dual carriageway to Sheppey built	*1995 AD*
Crematorium opened in Bobbing	*2003AD*

Bobbing and its heritage

Bobbing has a history as a relatively small agricultural village or parish which can be found approximately two miles to the north-west of the town of Sittingbourne. The centre of the village lies about three-quarters of a mile to the east from the main London to Dover Road - along the old Sheppey Way - which continues on to the north-east and to the village of Iwade.

Although first found on early maps dating from the 12th and 13th Century under the names of Bobinge, Bobbynge, Bobbing, Bobbinges, it is believed to take its name from a Celtic tribe that lived on the higher ground that was to the north of the fresh water marshes of the Meads and nearby creeks.

As far back as the time of the Roman occupation, Bobbing was a source of raw materials for the building of Watling Street through the parish as well as for chalk and brick making clay. Later the area was raided by foreign armies which included the Saxons, Vikings, Dutch and French.

For many years, Key Street – first recorded under the name of de Kaystre in the Assize rolls of 1226 and in 1254 as Kaystrete - was considered to be at the heart of the Bobbing village. Key Street and Chestnut Street were at that time part of the parish. Today, the north side of Key Street is in the parish of Bobbing, the south side in the parish of Borden, as is Chestnut Street.

Following the Norman Conquest, Bobbing became home to descendents of the Norman survivors of the Battle of Hastings and, over the next four hundred years, provided knights and army commanders that fought in The Crusades and major battles in Palestine, Scotland, the Caribbean and Ireland and who sailed with Francis Drake and Admiral Sir John Hawkins. MPs, Sheriffs, Justices of the Peace, Governors and landed gentry also came from Bobbing, while some received Royal Patronage or were friends of English Kings and Queens. A Royal hunting lodge was also to be found in the parish.

Even later, Bobbing was the birthplace of a passenger who sailed from Plymouth on the Ark – in company with the Dove - and who was to eventually become the second Governor of Maryland, naming his lands after his county and village of birth.

Throughout the centuries farming and agriculture were dominant in the village – particularly fruit growing and the growing of a variety of cereals. For almost 200 years there was a flour mill in the village at Bobbing Hill. Root crops also grew well on the loamy, arable soil.

The village church has been at the centre of the village since the early 13th Century and is believed to have been built in the reign of Henry II. Old brasses and monuments in the church help to record something of the village's history and gentry. A missionary foundation in Bobbing dates back to 670, while land in Bobbing was owned by Minster Priory as far back as 1186. An early chapel in the village was in use during Roman times.

Many advances and changes took place in the village during the 1800s – fresh water supply, an infectious diseases hospital, gas supply, the main London to Dover railway line, telegraph communications, education for all, and fire and ambulance services.

Being close to gun emplacements and barrage balloons at Chetney during World War II meant that Bobbing was close to the battle being fought over the skies in Kent. Dog fights, enemy planes shot down, parachutes dropping from the sky, all were part of Bobbing life in the 1940s. Children attending the local school often spent time having lessons in an air raid shelter attached to the school.

Today, Bobbing is a rather different place. Agriculture and farming have largely declined. A major new trunk road linking the M2 motorway and the Isle of Sheppey runs through part of the parish – relieving traffic in the village centre. The village school has been expanded and a number of new housing and commercial developments have been completed.

Undoubtedly the village will continue to evolve and change, but probably not to the extent it did in the past, or probably ever again to the level of Royal patronage, English and local government influence, or historical eminence that it once had.

This publication is intended to give something of the sense of history that a small village can have on a county. Indeed on the country as a whole and even on other countries as well. Bobbing is perhaps not unique, but its heritage and history is far more important than its size should ever justify. It is an interesting story.

Bobbing - one of the first tribal settlements

Prior to the Roman invasions of 55 and 54 BC the people who lived in the north and east of Kent, centred on Canterbury and stretching along the Thames estuary and Kent rivers and creeks, were the Cantiaci or Cantii tribesmen. Even before that, back to the Iron Age and the Stone Age, there is evidence of habitation and flint tools in this locality.

Largely of Celtic or even Teutonic origin, the tribesman were in a position to command trade between Britain and Gaul, exporting goods such as quality clothing - particularly the prized British woollen cloak - grain, cattle, iron and a range of other products to their Romanised neighbours across The Channel. In return, they received jewellery, wine, fine pots, metal work, and luxury goods they could not make themselves.

Early flint tools found at nearby Iwade. Photo courtesy of Sittingbourne Heritage Museum

The Cantii are believed to have already been using coinage for at least a hundred years or more - back to 150 BC - and were skilled in tilling land, growing crops and herding cattle. They were a relatively prosperous and civilized people, open to influences from France and the Mediterranean and often envied by those with whom they traded. Not unsurprisingly, they were frequently subjected to regular incursions by invading foreign armies and from European migrants looking for a better life and land (a familiar story still today). Some stayed longer than others, while some simply came to rape and pillage.

To protect themselves, the Kentish tribes banded together under local tribal leaders to defend themselves, their land, livestock and families. Frequently this was by building their individual settlements on higher ground surrounded by rivers and creeks, woodland, by marshland, or by building man-made forts and moats - again, often on higher ground. They were also capable warriors, ready and able to defend themselves.

No proper roads existed at this time and the only communication between the Kentish settlements was by horse, by walking or by driving cattle along trackways that followed natural contours in the land or safe routes through surrounding marshland. Having said this, they could rapidly band together if invasion threatened.

It is from this background of farming and security that the village and surroundings of Bobbing are believed to have derived. Using the Old English 'ingas' - a term used to describe people, followers or tribe of - Bobbing is believed to be the first and original settlement in England of a clan or tribe of people originally descended from 'Bobba', a Teutonic Northern European family.

Another branch of the same Bobba clan is believed to have settled in Normandy, France, while Roman records indicate that Bayeaux in Normandy is the place that was colonized by Loeti Bobba. Other clan members settled in central France and founded Bobigny – which is now a suburb of Paris. A further branch settled in Beaubigny, in Burgundy, France, on the eastern frontier of the Roman Province of Gaul.

This English Bobba or Bobbinga's settlement that developed as a late Iron Age farmstead is said to have been located on the higher ground of what is now known as Bobbing and is believed to have extended north from where the village church now stands.

The banks on the south-west side of the church at that time were largely of fertile farmland, while out towards the settlements that were also developing around Milton and Iwade, it was often difficult to traverse freshwater marshland (the Milton Meads), once believed to have been part of a stream or river winding down from Stockbury Valley, through the Meads and on to join up with Milton Creek, with the Swale and river Medway, Milton and numerous creeks, to the east and north. Much of the higher ground to the north-west and west of the settlement was oak and chestnut forests.

The Bobbinga tribe would therefore be relatively well protected from raids, were able to farm freely on land around the settlement which would have been cleared of forest and shrubs using hafted axes, could hunt in the nearby oak and chestnut forests and/or marshland,

Hafted Palstone axe of the type excavated locally.
Drawing by Michael Fairley

and fish in the various creeks and inlets. There is even the possibility of flint mining.

Houses of the Bobbinga tribe would most likely have been round with a conical, sloping thatched roof, all supported by poles set into the ground. This is supported by evidence from excavations at nearby Iwade where post holes were found in circles. Walls were usually made of woven twigs, which were then weatherproofed with clay daub. There was a doorway or entrance, but no windows.

Round house with conical thatched roof of the type built by the Bobbinga tribe.
Drawing by Michael Fairley

As time passed the community would have prospered and grown; probably village defences would have been built, and maybe even a small fort established. A community the size of a small village would have eventually developed.

Through trade with The Continent and, indirectly with Rome, the Romans would have been aware of the relative prosperity of some of these Kentish settlements and eventually, in 55 BC and again in 54 BC, expeditions were sent to report on whether it was worth making the south-east and eventually the rest of England, part of the Roman Empire.

These expeditions landed in Kent and came up the rivers and marshes of the Stour, Medway and Thames before they returned to Gaul to report, but not without first coming across fierce opposition from the Cantii tribes, which would undoubtedly have included the Bobbinga's, who were able to see off Caesar - causing mayhem among the Roman troops with chariot attacks and men on horseback for which the Romans had no battle plan, and chasing them back to the Roman boats waiting on the banks of the waterways. Outnumbered and outmanoeuvred, the enemy sailed back to Gaul

Following these early Roman invasions Britain and the Kentish tribes were largely left in peace for the next 100 years and continued to build trade with the Gauls and with Rome, until anti-Roman feelings in this south-east corner of Britain gave Emperor Claudius the excuse to refocus his energies on the country.

In AD 43 Claudius sent Aulus Plautius to Britain with some 40,000 Roman troops - four times the number in the original expeditions - to first conquer and then to occupy the country. Although various skirmishes took place, during which some of the Kentish tribal leaders were killed and other headed for Wales (it is not known what happened to the Bobba or Bobbinga tribe leaders), the inhabitants of Kent were eventually disarmed and Aulus Plautius was established as the first governor.

Familiar with the tribal boundary system, the Romans accommodated many of these boundaries into their own administrative organization. Canterbury, renamed Durovernum, was rapidly developed to become the tribal (and Roman) capital of Kent; while Rochester was developed to defend the Medway. Work was also started on the building of a extensive road network needed for military patrols and for communication between the new Roman settlements, and as supply routes to provide garrison forts with food and equipment and to trade goods.

At this time there is some evidence to indicate that originally the Romans may have used an old Celtic track that crossed Kent and ran through Iwade and Newington, north of where Watling Street was eventually built, and on to Rochester.

It is also known that in the parish of Borden, adjoining Bobbing to the south, a hill fort existed at the time of the Roman invasion. This fort was eventually taken over by the Romans not long after their arrival in Kent.

For the next 400 years Kent, and the area in and around Bobbing, were to be part of the Roman Empire. A new chapter in Bobbing's history and heritage had now begun.

Roman life comes to the village

One of the first requirements following the successful invasion and disarming of the Kentish tribes by the Romans was for them to build a key road network linking their new ports of Richborough, Dover and Lympe to the developing towns of Canterbury and Rochester and on to the capital in London. This road, called Watling Street by the Romans, needed to be straight and defensible, possibly administered and maintained from local forts.

This major new road network was initially for military purposes but soon also rapidly became essential for the movement of goods and people, for trading and exporting, and for communications. Major roads such as this needed to be fairly substantial, usable even in wet and bad weather conditions, able to carry heavy traffic and give some measure of protection to travellers.

With transport and communications at the heart of the Roman occupation, road building was an initial priority with a major route to be built between the Kentish capital and London, so putting Watling Street at or near the top of their list. This almost straight road linking Canterbury with London also incorporated by its side Roman settlements at Ospringe, Milton, Rochester and Dartford.

Supervised by military engineers, who sited this new road from hilltop to hilltop, the building of Watling Street would have required a ready supply of local tribal labour to clear the ground, excavate boundary trenches - which defined the width of the road, acted as defensive features and provided drainage - and to lay the road surface.

In many places up to 15 metres (45 feet) wide and constructed up to one or more metres (3 foot) in height, the road was predominately constructed with chalk flints, broken stones or blocks, and finally surfaced with gravel rammed hard to consolidate and form a camber for drainage. Bobbing and the surrounding area were therefore of major importance to the Romans.

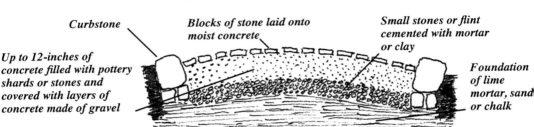

Diagram shows the basic construction of a Roman road of the type that came through Bobbing as Watling Street.
Drawing by Michael Fairley

Local flintstones from Chestnut Street, originally part of Bobbing, were used in the construction of Watling Street, while a gravel pit of an unusual length and depth - believed to have been made by the Romans for the top surfacing of the new highway - can still be seen about one mile along the old Detling Road. Gravel was also extracted from the Grove Park area.

Certainly, it is easy to see why the Romans chose this route to London; from the high ground at the top of Keycol Hill it would have been possible to see Boughton Hill to the East and Cuxton Hill to the west. The terrain would have been relatively easy to clear, being largely scrubland rather than forest. Building materials were plentiful and labour was available. It would also have been easy to defend, with military support from the sea being an option.

Add to that the ready supply of oak and chestnut timber from local forests for making the oxen carts used to transport the flint and gravel, and it seems likely that the Bobbing area would have housed some kind of Roman encampment of soldiers and engineers to supervise local inhabitants in quarrying and road building tasks. There is certainly evidence of such an encampment, with Roman remains being found close to Watling Street.

Evidence of Roman habitation has also been found at several nearby locations, including Iwade, as well as Romano-British cremation and burial sites within the parish boundaries and around the Sittinbourne area. Artifacts discovered in the area include bronze lamps, bronze ewers, Samian pottery, glass jugs, bronze jugs, finger rings and hair pins, brooches and spoons.

Samian ware Roman pottery from the Sittingbourne area. Photo courtesy of Sitting-bourne Heritage Museum

Those not set to work on road building activities would have been kept busy in developing the local farmland, cattle and crops to feed the soldiers and workers. All the Roman roads carried milestones, while posting houses were built along the major roads for the Roman postal service and official travellers.

Passing through the south-west side of Bobbing, Watling Street was soon to become a major route carrying heavy low-sided four-wheeled waggons pulled by oxen, two-wheeled mule carts with seats for one or two passengers, and even litters with rich people inside that were carried by slaves. For the people of Bobbing these sights would have been part of their daily life. Additionally, there would be frequent columns of Roman soldiers passing along the route to and from garrisons and on patrol.

Apart from the initial building of Watling Street, new local roads were being built in the Bobbing area to open up trade and to link the newly built and expanding farmland and estates in the area with local markets and towns. These local roads were not straight or to the standards of military roads, but tended to be upgraded routes following already existing ancient trackways or the contours of the countryside.

It is likely that the road from the Watling Street crossroads at Key Street (possibly from the Roman Caius Street or Casingc Street, or from Quay Street, where there was a wharf or quay on the river running down from Stockbury) ran through Bobbing and Iwade to the Isle of Sheppey. A road from Bobbing to Milton probably carried produce to the Milton market, and fish or oysters from the fishing fleet in Milton creek back to the village.

Local roads to the village or to Watling Street would also have been upgraded to carry the local black pottery from Upchurch, transport quarry materials in the area for buildings and roads, tiles, iron, woollen cloth, white limestone (for lining Roman baths) and bricks - all of which were produced in prosperous Kent at that time.

With Watling Street passing through Bobbing, it provided the opportunity for local trade with soldiers and merchants, selling food, drink or other goods to those passing along this great and busy highway. Life for many in Bobbing would have been quite settled and, for the times, quite prosperous.

As for the Romans, remains of up to 20 Roman villas or farmsteads – some quite large and luxurious and likely to have been the homes of Roman officials – have been uncovered between Chatham and Faversham and bordering or close to Watling Street. These officials would have lived in some comfort.

By the end of the second century traffic on Watling Street and through Bobbing had become so heavy that the Romans eventually banned the movement of heavy vehicles during daylight hours.

Roman occupation and villas along Watling Street. Illustration from a backdrop in Sittingbourne Heritage Museum

Heavy loads now had to be moved by night. Trade, through local hostelries by the side of the road, would now be carried on during the day and night. The first early inns at Key Street would have been in business for overnight travellers and the area around Key Street would have been quite a thriving community.

However, all good things are said to come to an end. In 401, the Romans withdrew many of their soldiers from Britain to help with the defence of Italy. To supplement the remaining soldiers, local Angles and Saxons were recruited as mercenaries. Probably some from Bobbing joined the Roman army in the area. Eventually, the remaining Romans were withdrawn.

Following this withdrawal, government and administrative links with Rome began to break down. Initially, nothing much changed, although the high standard of road maintenance on Watling Street would have ended and, with the Roman army much reduced, movement of goods and people on the highway would have been significantly lower; and with no major army to feed, the growth of farming and food production in the Bobbing area would have slowed.

A new era in Bobbing's history was about to begin.

The rise of the Kingdom of Kent

Although the Romanised Britons tried to maintain the high standards of administration, efficiency and security inherited from the Roman empire over 400 years, the county of Kent was soon coming under increasing pressure from invasions from the north of England and from the north-west of Europe. The Picts and the Scots constantly attacked into Kent while pagan hordes and foreign armies, including the Saxons and Vikings, were plundering the region.

Indeed it is believed that the name of Howte Green in Bobbing derives its origin from the Viking or Saxon period, with the Saxon name 'Bolt' meaning a wood ending up being translated as Holte or Howte. Certainly, the relatively peaceful, prosperous and civilised life of the past 400 years in Kent, and Bobbing, was coming to an end.

By the 5th century, the Saxon pirates were increasing their activities, as were the Picts and Scots while the British chieftains were having to contend with internal dissension. At that time Vortigern, a British ruler who held sway over much of southern England and Kent, invited the Jutish (a Low German tribe) chieftains Hengist and Horsa to come and help to defend the country which they did in 449.

Initially settling in Thanet, they soon extended their domain to all of Kent east of the Medway, becoming even more troublesome than the enemies they had come to contain. Then, turning against Vortigern, Hengist soon took control of all of Kent, plundering neighbouring counties and cities until he ruled over the whole of south-east England. Bobbing was now firmly under the rule of the Jutes. Indeed, the area became a Royal Jutish estate with a Palace in the neighbouring community of Milton. This extended from Upchurch to Tonge, including Bobbing.

It was during this period that the population of the area dropped and the forests again began to take hold, perhaps encouraged as part of the Royal estate. Certainly, there is no doubt that the area was again thickly wooded for a period in the Middle Ages.

By 488 Oisc, the son of Hengist, had become the first of the 'Saxon' kings of Kent, with the boundaries established at that time remaining almost unchanged to the present time. Later, in 560, the grandson of Oisc, Ethelbert, began his reign as King of Kent. It was under his reign that St. Augustine was welcomed to the county to convert the English to Christianity, building Saxon churches throughout Kent in the following years.

The church now took an increased role in the government and administration of the kingdom with skilled administrators and virtually all learning being provided by the church. Most of the best land in Kent was also now owned by the church and was farmed well and profitably by tenant landlords. Bobbing was part of the parish of Milton and, again, would probably have had tenant church farmers

Following a brief spell of paganism in the early 7th century, Christianity was restored to the county, only to be followed by a period of turmoil when Kent was divided amongst various minor kings until it was reunited for a time in 690 by the King of Mercia,

Wihtred. Kent then remained under the control of the kings of Mercia until they were defeated by Egbert, King of Wessex, in 825. Kent and the people of Bobbing now became a part of the rising kingdom of Wessex.

By 835 the Danes were beginning their raids into Kent, sacking both Rochester and Canterbury in 839. The Danes began their occupation by wintering on the Isle of Sheppey in 851/2 and over the next half-century laid waste to great areas of north and east Kent. Almost certainly this would have included Bobbing - alongside neighbour Milton, which is known to have been plundered by Hosten in 893 after a fleet of 350 Danish ships came up the Thames estuary and into Kent, albeit meeting resistance from King Alfred the Great, King of Wessex, whose troops were gathered at Bayford Castle, near Milton Creek.

Kent finally lost its status as a separate kingdom. It was now ruled by one king - the King of England. This lead to some stability until England was again invaded by the Danes in both 999 and 1013 with the aim of taking over the English throne. This they achieved under King Canute in 1016. Following his conversion to Christianity, Kent now had a relatively peaceful period after some 600 years of upheaval and turmoil, remaining under Saxon rule until King Harold's battle with Duke William of Normandy at Hastings in 1066.

Following the Norman Conquest, the newly crowned King William set out to take command of Dover Castle, only to be met on the way by an army of men offering allegiance to the King - but only on terms that enabled the ancient liberties and privileges of

Kent to once again be recognized. The alternative to not agreeing these terms would be a bloody resistance.

William therefore agreed that Kent could continue its Saxon traditions, upon which Dover Castle was surrendered to him. It also meant that Kent was to be the only county not actually defeated in battle by the Normans.

A new period in the history of Kent, and particularly Bobbing, was now underway.

The importance of Norman Bobbing

Following the Norman Conquest, King William began destroying some of the sprawling earldoms of his predecessor, Harold, replacing many of the Bishops and Earls of England with his own family, military chiefs and Norman friends. Odo, Bishop of Bayeux and William's half-brother, who had blessed the troops before the Battle of Hastings and also taken part in the battle, was rewarded by becoming the Earl of Kent and being granted the town of Dover, while Bishop Lanfranc became the Archbishop of Canterbury. Unlike the Saxons, who had come to England to farm, the Normans had come to rule.

Quite remorselessly, the French-speaking Normans quickly spread throughout the government and Churches of England – they already had the land. The King granted land to the Norman barons, who in turn let it to their knights and freemen, who let it to the peasants to work – both for themselves and for their lord.

In total, Odo acquired land in 23 counties of England, primarily in the southeast, where he had destroyed and plundered the landowners of Kent to forcibly sieze lands for his friends and family. Consequently, Odo became a huge landowner in Kent – holding some 184 lordships in the county in his favour. Indeed, according to the Domesday book, Odo was the richest tenant-in-chief in England.

Although Bobbing was not specifically mentioned in the Domesday book, much of the land nearby was: Milton Regis was the king's land and contained 6 mills, 27 salt houses and 32 fisheries; Upchurch, where the Romans had built a large pottery, was held by Hugh de Port from the Bishop of Bayeaux, as was Tonge; Stockbury was again Bishop of Bayeaux land while Newington was held by Albert the Chaplain.

Kent, like the rest of England, was now firmly under the rule of the Normans and French was to become the official language of the county for the next two hundred years. It was during this period of Norman rule that descendants of those who took part in the Battle of Hastings began to move into and build manorial houses in Kent, and in Bobbing – most notably the Savage family.

As noblemen of the Kings, the Savage family would probably already have known Bobbing, for it was one of the hunting grounds regularly used by Royalty - from Stephen in the mid 1100s through to King John in early 1200. Both were said to have been regular visitors to the moated and fortified Norwood Castle in the forest to the north of the parish, where they would have hunted deer and wild boar.

Believed to be directly descended in line from Thomas Le Savage (or Sauvage) of Normandy, Ralph de Savage is known to have come to Bobbing in the 12th century. His son, Roger Savage – later knighted as Sir Roger Savage – is recorded as being born in 1187 to Ralph and his wife, who were by then already living at Bobbing Court, which remained in the hands of the Savage family for over 200 years before Eleanor Savage – widow of Sir Arnold Savage of Bobbing Court married Sir William de Clifford in 1405. Bobbing Court was then in the hands of the Clifford family for several hundred years.

Thomas Le Sauvage himself had come from Normandy to England with William the Conqueror in 1066 and appears on the list of survivors of the Battle of Hastings. For his part in the Battle, Thomas was rewarded by King William with lands in Derbyshire and, over the next hundred years, the family branched out into a number of other English counties, and even into Ireland. The Savage name is subsequently found amongst the crusaders, knighted warriors, speakers of the House of Commons, Bishops and Archbishops and even as poets.

Certainly within little more than a hundred years of arriving in England the Savage family were already very eminent, had Royal patronage and possessed many estates in Kent, including the manor of Bobbing. The manor house at Bobbing Court, home to Ralph de Savage, was a large building, which was adjacent to where the church now stands and is believed to be on the site of the current village school. It was eventually demolished in 1748

Ralph de Savage – who is said to have purchased Bobbing Court from the Molynes family - was present with King Richard I at the siege of Acon in Palestine between 1190 and 1194. Some of his descendents, Sir John de Savage, Sir Thomas de Savage, of Bobbing, and Sir Roger de Savage were later with King Edward I at the great siege of Caerlaverock Castle (situated near the salt marshes of the Solway Firth in Scotland) in 1300, where all three were dubbed with knighthoods and invested with a coat of arms for service to the king. The arms of the Savage family, six lions

The arms of the Savage family, six lions rampant

rampant sable, can still be seen on the roof of the cloisters of Canterbury Cathedral.

During the reign of King Edward II, archive documents show that Roger de Savage possessed the manor of Bobbing, 'obtaining free-warren and other liberties for his lands in Bobbynges, Middleton, Borden, Newenton and Stokebury.'

In 1359, Joan Savage of Bobbing Court married Ralph St. Leger. He was knighted in 1377 and eventually became Chancellor of the Exchequer of the 2nd Parliament in the reign of King Richard II. Prior to that he was sent on the 'affairs' of King Edward III to Gascony after the signing of the treaty between France and England. He was also Sheriff of Kent in 1347 and three times a Member of Parliament.

The manor continued in the Savage family down to Sir Arnold Savage, who was made a lifetime constable of the Royal Queenborough Castle (commenced in 1361 and demolished around 1650) in 1386 and twice became Speaker of the House of Commons during Henry IV's time. He was born at Bobbing Court in 1358 and, as he was a minor at the time of his parents' death, he was made a Royal Ward and subsequently a squire in the household of Richard II. He was appointed a Justice of the Peace in Kent and, after being knighted in 1385, became Sheriff of Kent.

He later joined the maritime force of the Earl of Arundel, contributing a further knight, some 28 esquires and 36 archers. To provide such a force it would have been necessary for the knights and archers to have been well trained and to have tested their skills at jousting and other tournaments, and through the use of a Quintain

– a post set in the ground with a revolving arm on top. On one end of the arm is a shield or target; on the other a heavy weight. Once struck by a contestant, the revolving arm would spin and, if the rider was too slow, he would be hit on the back or head by the weight. It is believed that this is where the name of Quinton (Quintain) Lane on the outskirts of Bobbing originated.

King Richard subsequently retained Sir Arnold as a King's Knight and made him Knight of the Shire of Kent in 1390. He died in 1410. Brasses to Sir Arnold and his wife Joan can be seen in Bobbing Church (beneath which lies the body of Sir Arnold). Following his death, his sister Eleanor, Baroness Cobham – who had first been married to Sir Reginald Cobham (with whom she had no children) and was at that time married to Sir William Clifford – became his rightful heir and inherited Bobbing Court – but now under the Clifford name.

A younger branch of the Clifford family had already been settled in Bobbing for some years at Bobbing Place. Indeed, a Walter Clifford is recorded as being one of the Domesday Commissioners. The arms of the Cliffords of Bobbing can be seen on the roof of the cloisters of Canterbury Cathedral, and in St Margarets Church in Canterbury. Like

Sir Arnold Savage, Knight, of Bobbing, clad in Lancastrian armour.

25

the Savage family, the Cliffords were from a long line of nobility and were distinguished warriors.

Sir William Clifford, like Sir Arnold Savage before him, was also to become Sheriff of Kent (twice in the 4th and 13th years of the reign of King Henry VI) and eventually died in 1438 leaving two sons, Lewis and John, both born at Bobbing Court. John married Margaret Gainsford and a son, William Clifford, in turn married Florence St. Leger – from another leading Kent family.

Lewis Clifford married Mildred Bourne (daughter of Bartholomew Bourne of Sharsted). Their son, Richard de Clifford – who had five children, including Catherine de Clifford, born at Bobbing Court in 1543 (and whose portrait can be seen in Maidstone museum) - was the grandfather of Sir Nicholas de Clifford, knighted by the Earl of Essex at Rouen in 1591, who had been born at Bobbing Court in 1563 to Sir Henry Clifford

Photograph of Catherine Clifford of Bobbing Court from a portrait painting in Maidstone Museum.

and Anne Devereux and was also grandfather to Sir Conyers de Clifford (born 1565, again knighted at Rouen in 1591), the son of George de Clifford and Mary Southwell. Nicholas sold Bobbing

Court to Sir Thomas Neville, but Richard Clifford repurchased it. After he died it passed to his son George.

Records in the Canterbury Archives dated in 1565 show George Clifforde, gentleman of Bobbing Court and son of Richard de Clifford; Ursula (nee Finch of Grovehurst), his bedfellow; James Drydale as his manservant and Jaen his wife, with Maryon Wolly as the maidservant. George and Ursula had 10 children – Henry, Alexander, Conyers, Lewis, Richard, Clement, George, Elizabeth, Mary and Catherine - while living at Bobbing Court.

After this, later, George de Clifford died his widow Mary became the second wife of Sir Anthony St Leger, Knight (knighted in 1593), Master of the Rolls and of his Majesty' Privy Council of Estate in the realm of Ireland. On his death in 1612 he left £10 to the poor of the parishes of Boughton Monchelsea, Bobbing and Bridge and £500 to his stepson, Conyers de Clifford of Bobbing Court.

When Mary died she divided Bobbing Court and manor in equal shares to her two sons, Henry and Conyers Clifford from her first marriage, and to her son Anthony St. Leger from her second marriage. They quickly sold the manor to Edward, Duke of Cosington who, not long after, passed it to Sir Richard Gurney, before it subsequently came back to the Clifford family.

Conyers de Clifford of Bobbing subsequently became the most famous Clifford in Ireland. A Governor of Connaught and Privy Councillor of Ireland, he was made – as already stated - a Knight in the Visitation of Rouen by the Earl of Essex. His Coat of Arms was on display in Queenborough Castle.

In April 1599, the Earl of Essex landed in Ireland with over 17,000 troops and cavalry to put down a rebellion which had spread from Ulster to all Ireland. Sir Conyers Clifford, an experienced army commander – then based in Athlone – was sent to relieve a besieged Collooney Castle with a force of 1,500 English infantry and 200 horse. On the way he was ambushed by musketeers, archers and javelin men in the Curlew Mountains. The further the English advanced, the more intense was the rebel fire. Eventually the main English column broke and fled. Although Clifford managed to rally the troops he was killed by a pike thrust as he rushed the enemy.

The Irish rebels cut off the head of Clifford and it was taken to Collooney Castle to intimidate the defenders, while the trunk was taken to Trinity Island and the monastery of Lough Key where it was buried.

Nicholas Clifford (Clyfford) of Bobbing, the cousin of Conyers Clifford, was also knighted by the Earl of Essex at Rouen and his Coat of Arms was again displayed in Queenborough Castle. He married Frances Drury, daughter of Sir William Drury of Hawstead. One of Queen Elizabeth's more professional commanders he sailed from Plymouth in 1595 with Admiral Sir John Hawkins and Sir Francis Drake in a fleet of 36 ships to fight the Spanish in the Caribbean. Dropping anchor at Porte Rico, the ships were attacked by ordnance from the mounts and, at supper-time, Sir Nicholas Clifford was mortally shot and died shortly after.

The Clifford family were to continue living at Bobbing Court until it was sold by another Nicholas Clifford to Sir Thomas

Neville. It was later re-purchased by Nicholas's younger son, Richard, and then remained with the Clifford family for a further four generations until finally being sold to Sir William Geary of Oxenhoath, who already held considerable lands in Bobbing and was the owner of the manor of Upper Toes (Uppertoes).

The American connection

Only a few years after the period in which the Clifford cousins were fighting (and dying) with the Spanish in the Caribbean and the Irish in the Curlew Mountains, a Thomas Greene was being born in Bobbing.. The second son of Sir Thomas Greene, whose great-grandfather had received the Rectory of Bobbing from Henry VIII upon the dissolution of the monasteries – and who was in turn the son of Sir Robert Greene - baby Thomas was eventually destined to become the second Governor of Maryland in the USA.

As a young man, he was to become one of the twenty gentlemen investors who were chosen to sail with the Ark and The Dove to seek a better life in the New World. Many of the 200 or so passengers on the ships were Catholics (as was Thomas Greene) looking to escape religious persecution and also, in his case, to avoid paying the excessive taxation imposed on manor lords, on some 10,000 acres of manor land (much of it in Bobbing) which he had earlier inherited.

Amongst those listed on the passenger manifesto of these two ships were 17 Catholic gentlemen, three Jesuit priests and around 200 Protestants and Catholics. A small number of the passengers were women. Part of the requirement was that all passengers on board, whatever their religion, should work and live in peace and unity both during the voyage and after they had settled in America where each adult would be granted 100 acres, every child 50 and indentured servants, who were also on the voyage, were to receive personal supplies and food.

Most passengers were carefully chosen from among people who could be important to the success of colony that they would found in the New World, including farmers to provide food, brick layers and carpenters to build houses, blacksmiths, shipbuilders and even some soldiers.

Part of the challenge of financing and planning the voyage was the need to take not only enough food for a voyage of four or five months but also to keep the settlement alive before they could grow food after they had arrived. In addition, all kinds of tools were needed for building, farming and furniture making, as well as guns, knives and swords for protection on route and hunting when they arrived. Then there was a need for both summer and winter clothing, plus all kinds of seeds and plant cuttings. Consequently, few passengers had cabins.

The two vessels were financed by the second Lord Baltimore (Cecil Calvert, also a Roman Catholic) following a charter originally granted by James I and then acceded to by Charles I after the death of James. The charter was for the establishment of a new colony of Maryland on the eastern shore of Chesapeake Bay; a dream long pursued by the 1st Baron Baltimore, and which was to be a refuge for English Catholics. Leonard Calvert, younger brother of Lord Baltimore, was named as the governor of the new lands.

The charter gave Baltimore and his descendents rights nearly equal to those of an independent state and included the rights to wage war, collect taxes, and establish a Colonial nobility. It also emphasized the importance of religious toleration among the new colonists, who were split almost equally in number between Catholics and Protestants.

Originally leaving Gravesend in mid-October 1633, they initially sailed for the Isle of Wight but not before they had first been chased down and brought back by the British navy to take an oath of allegiance to the King. At the Isle of Wight they picked up additional passengers before finally setting sail for America on the 22nd of November 1633 – St Cecilia's day. The plan was to take a southwesterly course to Barbados then sail northwards up the coast of America.

Within a few days the two ships encountered a major storm and the Dove disappeared, believed foundered. It had in fact turned back to England to wait out the storm, and then continued at a later date. The Ark sailed on alone, arriving in Barbados on 3rd January 1634 where they decided to rest and take on fresh supplies. Three weeks later, much to the Ark's surprise, the Dove also arrived.

From Barbados the two ships sailed on to Point Comfort in Virginia where they presented letters from the King and Chancellor of the Exchequer to the Governor of Virginia. Re-supplied, the two ships sailed north through Chesapeake Bay and into the Potomac River.

Part of an early map of Maryland and Chesapeake Bay where the Ark and the Dove sailed. Kent Island is arrowed.

Finally, after more than four months sailing, they arrived at St Clements's Island in present-day St. Mary's County, Maryland, on March 25th 1634. Even today, this date is celebrated as Maryland Day.

The Island served as a convenient temporary base of operations for the settlers and, after several days exploring they found a suitable area of land for settlement on Kent Island, the largest island in Chesapeake Bay, for which they purchased the land from the Yaocomico Indians. Changing the name to St. Mary's City they started to build houses from cut wood and with shingled roofs. Soon, they were also building brick houses and by the late 1670s, St. Mary's City – Maryland's first capital – had many fine buildings and houses. It was also to become one of the predominately catholic regions among the English colonies in America.

Maryland also became a key destination for tens of thousands of British convicts punished by sentences of transportation – long before convicts were transported to Australia.

It was not long after landing in Maryland that Thomas Greene married Ann Cox, one of the few gentlewomen on the voyage of the Ark and the Dove. This is believed to have been the first ever Christian marriage to be celebrated on Maryland soil. She died, after having borne two sons within a few years, after which he later married Winifred Seyborne with whom he had two further sons.

In 1645, Lord Baltimore granted Thomas Greene a manor of 500 acres on the tip of Kent Isle, Maryland – not far from Fort Kent Manor. Greene gave the name of Bobbing (after his ancestral estate in Kent) to his island manor with court Baron and held it until

1651, when he sold it for 10,000 lbs of tobacco. He received other land grants, one for 2,500 acres which was eventually granted to his three sons in 1656 and named 'Greene's Inheritance.'

Thomas Greene had a keen interest in the affairs of the Province. He attended General Assemblies and was one of the first to be appointed to the Lord Proprietary of the Upper Council or Privy Council, an equivalent counterpart to the House of Lords in England. A Justice of the Provincial Court, he retained his seat in the Council until 1647 when he succeeded Leonard Calvert, the first Provincial Governor, on his death in 1647.

Thomas Greene served as Provincial Governor of Maryland until 1649 and died in 1651.

The Maryland colony of Calvert and Greene was established as a place where Christians of all different faiths could live in unity and religious tolerance became the official policy of Maryland. So too, did recognition of the native American Indians as a separate people with their own rights. These two pieces of progressive policy foreshadowed the provisions of the US Constitution which guaranteed the separation of the church and state and laws to protect civil rights.

Religion and the Church

When the Romans came to England they had a great toleration towards other (pagan) gods and there was undoubtedly some merging of Roman and Celtic religious beliefs. The only religion they disapproved of was Druidism, which they suppressed. Christianity became the official religion of England during the later part of the Roman occupation.

At that time, religious services were carried out in private houses and villas that were built by the Romans were made to accommodate a place of worship with the walls decorated in Christian subjects. With a Roman villa at Milton and others along Watling Street, evidence of a Roman settlement in the Bobbing area and regular travel by noblemen, soldiers and traders along Watling Street, it is certain that their form of Christianity would have been practiced in Bobbing.

Indeed a number of Romano-British cremation sites have been found in the area, including at Bobbing and Iwade, as well as Roman burial sites and a Roman cemetery around Milton. These cremation and burial sites were outside the areas of residence.

The task of converting the inhabitants of Kent to Roman Catholic Christianity was later led by Augustine, an Italian Bishop who landed in Kent in 597. King Ethelbert accepted this new faith and Augustine became the first Archbishop of Canterbury. Over the next 100 years Christianity spread to most of England.

Sexburga, a daughter of the king of East Angles, married Ercombert, king of Kent and, after his death in 664 she ruled the kingdom until her son was old enough to take over. Around 670, she founded a nunnery in Sheppey, endowed it and lived there with her disciples. After she died, Sexburga was canonized – eventually to share this dedication with St Mary. This nunnery or priory, was eventually to play a significant role in the history of Bobbing.

It was also in the seventh century that the Minster Church of Milton was founded, from which priests travelled to spread the faith in the surrounding areas. Missionary foundations were established in Tunstall, Bobbing, Sittingbourne, Bredgar and Borden. These established local churches owed their allegiance to the founding Minster and, as such, nearby Milton developed to become the main community in the area. Such was its level of importance that it was eventually afforded royal status – hence the name of Milton Regis.

The church now took an increased role in the government and administration of the kingdom, with skilled administrators and virtually all learning being provided by the church. Most of the best land in Kent was also now owned by the church and was farmed well and profitably by tenant landlords. Bobbing, as part of the parish of Milton at that time, would have had tenant church farmers

Following a brief spell of paganism in the early 7th century Christianity was again restored to the county only to be followed by a period of turmoil when Kent was divided amongst various minor kings until it was reunited for a time in 690 by the king of Mercia, Wihtred.

When William the Conqueror seized England it was with the

Pope's blessing and he soon sought to order the English Church. Through Archbishop Lanfrac, dioceses and cathedral chapters were organized, Church Courts and Church Law were developed – with new Norman churches built enthusiastically. Bishops, who were often barons in their own right, frequently held the Church's lands in trust from the king.

Certainly Roger, Abbot of St. Augustine's, Canterbury, gave certain tithes in the parish of Bobbing (for a rent of 10 shillings a year) to Agnes, prioress of Minster Priory in Sheppey in 1186. This priory – as mentioned earlier – had been established in Minster in about 670. There was also a monastery in Newington at the end of the 11th century in which there were a number of nuns believed to be from Minster. Records also show that Bobbing church and tithes were given to the Benedictine Priory at Minster in 1234 by King Henry III

Sir Roger de Northwode of Bobbing (the husband of Eleanor Savage of Bobbing) who died in 1286 and is buried before the altar of the Priory is said to have helped to relieve the poverty of Minster Priory – which had at that time fallen into ruin – while in 1303 a licence was granted to the prioress and nuns to acquire land from Henry de Northwode to find a chaplain to celebrate divine service daily in their church.

The Northwode or Norwood family – are believed to have originated in Kent where Sir Stephen de Northwoode, son of Jordanus de Sheppey, first adopted the Norman style surname after the 'north woods' of his estate some time between 1177 and 1231 – later became lords of the manor of Milton Regis.

The tax rolls of that time recorded that four months after the succession of King John (1199), Stephen de Northwode had his grants from King Richard I reconfirmed by King John. He paid 100 shillings in September 1200 for the reconfirmation.

The Norwood family can also take great credit for the restoration and new building work on Milton's Holy Trinty Church in the early 14th century.

Later, in 1340, Archbishop John de Strafford confirmed the appropriation to the priory of churches belonging to it. The covenant produced as evidence for the church of Minster letters of John de Peckham, archbishop, mentioning that he had inspected letters and muniments (title deeds preserved as evidence of rights or privileges) of William and Theobold, archbishops, for grants for the church of Bobbing from King Richard and St John.

While there appears to be no exact record of when the Church of St. Barthlomew, Bobbing, was actually built it was certainly existing and appropriated to Minster Priory according to the archbishop's documents of 1340. Indeed, it is first said to have been given by Henry III in his 18th year of reign (around 1234) to the Priory of St Mary and St Sexburgh in the Isle of Sheppey. This was later confirmed by Henry IV in his 1st year of reign by his letters and continued until the dissolution of religious houses in the 27th year of Henry VIII.

Even prior to Henry III's time, there is evidence that the church was built on the ruins of a previous (Saxon?) church or chapel on the site. This would seem to tie in with the period of building churches undertaken by the Normans. The Savage family would undoubtedly have worshipped in some form of chapel when they inhabited Bobbing Court in the 1100s while Agnes, prioress of Sheppey, was given tithes from Bobbing in 1188.

There was certainly a chaplain of Bobbing in 1243 who is shown as witnessing a grant to the hospital of the Holy Cross in Sittingbourne at that time. After Thomas Becket was murdered at Canterbury Cathedral in 1170 there were regular passages of pilgrims along Watling Street and there is known to have been a Chapel on the south side of Key Street for them to worship. The chapel was used by pilgrims for prayers and overnight accommodation. It is thought that it stood where the present 'Dental Terrace' – erected during the Victorian era – stands today.

The Chapel, known as St. James at Dental (a field mentioned in the will of Alexander Clyfford in 1494), was built by the Savage family of Bobbing Court. It was part of the Manor of Bobbing and the right to appoint a priest or master there belonged to the Lord of the Manor, just as the right to appoint the Vicar of Bobbing did. St James was the patron saint of pilgrims. Services were held in the Chapel in the summer during the pilgrimage season. It was closed in the winter. The Chapel was still functioning in 1526 but is believed to have become a hospital in the late sixteenth or early seventeenth century and was known as the Key Street Spittlehouse.

In 1605 an agreement was made between Richard Sherwyn, the governor or master of St James at Dental, and the town of Maidstone. By this bond Maidstone sent a Thomas Binks, 'a poor blinde and impotent creature' to the hospital. The last known record of this hospital occurred in 1607 when an epileptic girl from Tong Parish, Ann Radolphe, was admitted. The building must have been quite small as the required number of inhabitants was said to have been just four people.

According to the monastic Britain map there was also a Monastic House Hospital for lepers in Chestnut Street sometime before 1256. This was a lesser hospital with a net annual income of less than £500 and was dissolved or moved elsewhere before 1500. No other information seems to be available.

As for Bobbing Church, this was built of flint in the Early English and Decorated styles, and is now believed to date from the middle part of the reign of Henry II (1216-1272). A great builder and supporter of the arts, Henry spent much of his time building or re-building cathedrals and churches (including Westminster Abbey which was his greatest memorial).

Nowhere near as old or big as the nearby church of Holy Trinity, Milton (later Milton Regis) which is first dated from around the middle of the 7th century and then re-built/restored and re-dedicated in 1070 after being burnt by Earl Godwin in 1052, Bobbing church had two aisles, two chancels and a western tower supporting a spire and contained 200 seats.

In Grayling's 'The churches of Kent' published in 1913, it states that there was originally a 13th century nave and chancel. During the second quarter of the 14th century the north wall was under-set with octagonal pillars and arches of rag stone, the capitals well moulded. The windows are all 14th century in the body of the building. The east window of the chancel is reticulated with carefully restored tracery by Hussey and which contains a good modern glass painting by Thomas Curtis.

The tower is plain with 13th century lancet windows seen over well- designed 14th century west windows. Interestingly, a painting of Bobbing Church in 1807 shows it with a tall steeple on top of the tower. It is not known exactly when this was removed, but records seem to indicate this was in the early 1800s.

One of the oldest and best possession of Bobbing church is said to be a sedilia – stone seats for priests in the south wall of a chancel – of which the capitals and bases are in the style of the 12th/13th century. The western column is carved and at the top of this stands two figures, one a mitred bishop and one of a clerk. It is believed that the sculpture shows St Martial, Archbishop of Limoges, ordaining a deacon. This is said to date from the mid-twelfth century, although it has also been suggested that the stone was brought in as part of a load of broken stones. However, overall, the church belongs to the Gothic decorated period. There are also some fragments of 14th century stained glass in the north window.

The church contains four brasses, one of which shows a handsome

Monumental brass of Sir Arnold Savage and Joan his wife, of Bobbing Court, in Bobbing Church

canopied portrait of Sir Arnold Savage and Lady Joan Savage, dated 1420. These incorporated two shields; one bearing the arms of Sir Arnold and the other the arms of Lord William Echingham, father of Lady Joan. These brasses were wrongly removed from the north chancel and placed on the tower wall according to registers of 1560. Today, they are somewhat damaged and not of their best.

Also from the 15th century there is a small brass in the church of Joan Bourne who died in 1496. She was the sister of the wife of Lewis Clifford of Bobbing Court.

In 1535, Minster Priory and Bobbing are mentioned in the Taxation of that year when the gross value of the Priory's possessions - including the manors of Minster, 'Upberye' in Gillingham and Pistock in Rodmersham, the parsonages of Gillingham, Grain, Bobbing and Minster, and the chapel of Queenborough - was said to be £173.9s.3½d, and the net value £129.7s.10½d.

Bobbing church continued in the possession of Minster Priory until 1536 when, after Henry VIII – originally a staunch defender of the Catholic orthodoxy – had been unable to obtain from the Pope a divorce from his wife Catherine, he appointed himself as the supreme head of the Church of England and dissolved or closed down the abbeys, nunneries and friaries of England. At this time Minster Priory was suppressed as 'not being of the clear yearly value of £200.

In 1540 the Diocese of Canterbury records show that Wilhelmus Maye was the then vicar of Bobbing. Diocese records also show that a Bobbing Church of England School was started in the same year. Later records show that the village schoolmaster, the vicar at that time, from 1607 to 1628 was a Franciscus Reynoldes. This is around the time (1612) that John Speed produced his map of Kent. Based on this, the section around Bobbing, Sittingbourne and Milton shows all the churches in the area.

Churches in Bobbing and the surrounding area based on a John Speed map of 1612.

Vicars throughout these earlier years are recorded as:

1540 – Wilhelmus Maye

1607 – Thomas Shawe

1607 – Franciscus Reynoldes

1630 – Am May

1635 – John Reader

1663 – William Scarlett

1673 – Titus Otes (six months)

1689 – Thomas Conway

1690 – Robert Philpott

1703 – John Napleton

1712 – John Burman

1726 – Richard Fleycher

1753 – Isaac Priest

1757 – Joseph Parry

Not that long after the dissolution, Henry VIII granted the tenancy of Bobbing church to Thomas Green, who became the tenant for a yearly rental of £12. At this time the tithes were passed into lay hands. Indeed, Kent Quarter Session records of 1608 certify that Thomas Green of Bobbing, his wife Margarett and Francis Greene, his mother, 'come to church when at home'. Several generations later it was another Thomas Greene of Bobbing who, being a Catholic and looking to escape religious persecution, sailed to America and became Governor of Maryland.

On 28th March 1610 Sir Thomas Norton of Bobbing went to the Archdeaconry Court regarding the description of a space in Bobbing Church allotted for the construction of a family pew.

Slightly earlier, in 1573, Archbishop Parker issued a commission followed by a proclamation from Queen Elizabeth, reflecting severely on the neglect of the bishops to keep all the churches in their diocese in 'a uniform and Godly order.' The commission report said:

'there was in this parishe a minister that contracted hym selfe

unto a widowe there called Anne Becketts, and upon hope of marriage she solde that wyc she had and went with hym and nowe hath left her and she is come to there parishe againe confessinge that in the hope of marriage she laid with him. They have had but one sermonde this year.'

However, even this scandal compares little with that of the infamous Titus Oates who was preferred to the vicarage of Bobbing on 7th March 1673. Referred to as 'the most illiterate dunce, incapable of improvement' during his time at Caius College, Cambridge, he had somehow slipped into Holy Orders prior to moving to Bobbing.

He left Bobbing the following year with a licence for non-residence and a reputation for dishonesty to act as a curate in Hastings where he brought a trumped up charge against William Parker, the schoolmaster. For this he was ejected from his living and was sent to prison. Escaping, he procured an appointment as chaplain on board a king's ship. Bobbing church records simply say 'Our Minister is gone to sea'.

It was Oates who, in 1678, fabricated the stories of the conspiracy of the Popish Party against the life of His Sacred Majesty, the Government and the Protestant Religion, of which the chief item tells of a design to assassinate the King. In total, sixteen innocent men were executed in direct connection with the Plot and eight priests were brought to the scaffold in the persecution of Catholics which followed from it.

Oates was later tried for perjury and condemned to be whipped, degraded, pilloried and imprisoned for life. He later obtained a

Document signed by Titus Oates, Vicar of Bobbing in 1673.

Royal Pardon and a pension which was withdrawn in 1693 at the instance of Queen Mary. However, Kent Quarter Sessions have records of a Titus Otes, vicar, as being the plaintiff in which the defendant, a William Poole, presented a document signed by Otes appointing Poole his attorney and collector of tithes for Bobbing.

Apart from the records relating to Titus Oates (Otes), Bobbing Church continued to add to its history and monuments during the 17th century. On the north wall of the nave are monuments of Henry and Elizabeth Sandford.

Raised by their three youngest surviving daughters in 1660, the inscription mentions that he served three kings, 'save in the late years of anarchy' when,

Monument to Henry and Elizabeth Sandford on the north wall of Bobbing Church.

apparently, he chose to part with his office rather than his loyalty.

Facing this proud couple, on the south wall of the nave, are the brothers Charles and Francis Tufton but shown as twins although Charles was born in 1636 and Francis in 1628. They were the sons of Sir Humphrey Tufton of Bobbing Court who is buried in the chancel.

Also in the chancel – on the south wall – is a latin plaque to William Tyndale who died in 1748. William was the son of a Thomas Tyndale who had purchased Bobbing Court from Col.

Robert Crayford, Governor of Sheerness Fort in the reign of King William IV. It was William Tyndale who pulled down the old Bobbing Court in 1748.

Photograph of a watercolour painting of 1807 showing Bobbing Church with a spire. Illustration courtesy Kent Archeological Society

Records from 1760 show there were 5 bells in the tower but by 1804 it is recorded that the tower and shingled spire had become 'so ruinous and dangerous a state that a thorough repair therefore and a new handing of the bells was necessary and that a new bell should be added'. At this time the bells were transported up the Thames, recast, and transported back (at a cost of £6.6s). A new bell frame and the repair of the shingled spire cost £45. 7s.6d.

A further inspection of the tower in 1919 again found serious damage, with masonry breaking away. It was recommended that all ringing of the church bells should be stopped because it was damaging the tower. It was not until 1935 that further work to secure the tower and bells was undertaken. The tenor bell was recast at this time with all the repair work and the recast bell costing £247 .8s.0d.

Various bequests have traditionally been associated with Bobbing Church. Every year since 1833 successive vicars of Bobbing distributed loaves of bread to parishioners on St. Valentines Day –

usually following a short service in the church. This strange bequest was made by the widow of Valentine Simpson. The bread was purchased from the annual income of a piece of land.

Customs of this sort at Bobbing were not unusual. In 1688 a Thomas Woollett made a bequest that £1 should be distributed to the poor of Bobbing each year. With the fall in the value of the pound over the years this bequest was later merged with that of the Valentine Simpson bequest.

Even earlier in the history of the church the Mary Gibbon bequest had been founded in Bobbing in 1678. This bequest provided that bibles should be given to children following the end of the term when they left Bobbing School. The bibles were distributed by the vicar on the second Sunday in Advent.

As far as the churchyard is concerned, this was extended to its present size in 1885 during the time of the Rev. Simpson, although it was not until 1910 under the Rev. Wall that a layout plan of the graves was started. This delay caused difficulties in identifying earlier graves. Vicars during the period from the early 1880s to the 1950s include:

1881 – W Ottley

1883 – R Simpson

1887 – E Westall

1899 – R Moor

1908 – S Townley

1909 to 1950 – R Wall

The Sittinbourne, Milton & District Directory of 1908/9 records that the living in Bobbing is a vicarage of the yearly net value of

£70, with half an acre of glebe – a portion of land attached to a clergyman's benefice. The living at that time was 'in the gift of the Rev. Henry G Hilton-Simpson, of Oxford, who is the Lord of the Manor.'

Within Bobbing churchyard the oldest gravestone dates back to 1611. Another one carries a carving of a skull and crossbones and is dated 1679. Other, much later gravestones, are for the Wall family. These include the Reverend Richard Wall - who served as the vicar of St. Bartholemew's for 41 years from 1909 - and his son, a Captain in the Grenadier Guards, who was killed by a Doodlebug flying bomb which exploded killing 117 other members of the congregation in the Guards Chapel, Wellington Barracks, in June 1944.

Apart from Bobbing Church, there were three Methodist chapels nearby in the parish of Borden; two at Key Street and one at Ode Street. The Primitive Methodist Chapel in Key Street was closed before the First World War. The Key Street Wesleyan Chapel was opened in 1867 and had room for 200 people. It was demolished in 1966, although the foundation stone is still in place, being left there when the rest of the building was pulled down

Bobbing Village Church photographed in 2007 by Michael Fairley

plate 1

Stained glass window in Bobbing Church. Photograph by Michael Fairley

plate 2

Farming through the ages

While woodland and forests covered more than half of Kent in prehistoric times, this was gradually cleared over hundreds of years to provide increased farming and agriculture. Even as far back as 6000 BC there were believed to be settled farming communities in Kent and by the late Iron Age (700-300BC) much of the best farming land was already under cultivation.

Even before the Romans invaded, the Kentish tribes around Bobbing were known to have been skilled in tilling land, growing crops and herding cattle, while the woodlands of Kent had already been reduced to perhaps 40-45% of the county.

By 150BC the banks on the south-west side of the road where Bobbing church now stands were already largely fertile farmland, while out towards the settlements that were developing around Milton and Iwade, it was often difficult to traverse freshwater marshland (the Milton Meads), with the Swale and river Medway, and numerous creeks, to the east and north. Much of the higher ground to the north-west and west of the settlement however was still forested.

The Bobbinga tribe that is said to give the village its name would therefore have been relatively well protected from raids, were able to farm freely, could hunt in the nearby oak and chestnut forests and/or marshland, and fish in the various creeks and inlets. They would drag ploughs in a criss-cross pattern over relatively small fields to sow and produce various types of cereals, from wheat and barley, to oats and rye. Even the practice of crop rotation was by then becoming common.

In addition, they were also believed to have grown peas and beans, lentils, as well as flax for clothing. Cattle, pigs and goats were kept for milking, and for food and clothing. These animals would have been slaughtered in the autumn and the meat smoked to preserve it. The skins were used for shoes and clothes, while wool was used for weaving. Dogs were kept for hunting, horses for racing and warfare, and even chickens were kept for food and eggs.

When the Romans arrived in the Bobbing area there was a need for extra food to feed the army and the workers who were building Watling Street, rather than just to feed the local villagers. Growing food now actually became a money making occupation aided by Roman advice on intensive crop production, crop rotation and cattle breeding. New crops were introduced from Europe as well as the herbs that the Romans needed for their cooking, and the small farming community in Bobbing would soon have been able to begin to build bigger houses.

Drink at this time would have largely been beer made from barley, or mead, a honey-based drink which was rather stronger than beer. The Romans also imported wine and, eventually, were able to grow grapes in Kent for wine making. Shops were set up to sell pottery and containers for food and for the olive oil that was imported.

It was from this early background that farming and agriculture became dominant in village life. By the time the Anglo Saxons invaded Kent (450 to 800AD) many agricultural estates had already been established – some dating as far back as Roman times and many controlled by kings – and rural inhabitants (the peasants and serfs) were employed in farming.

Farm implements at this time would have been a either a hand plough or a ploughshare pulled by oxen, an iron sickle with long wooden handle for reaping of cereals and an iron axe for clearing undergrowth. Clothing would have consisted of a shirt and breeches, leggings and leather shoes – together with an outer garment. The clothing would have been made from home-woven cloth.

Reaping of cereals in Saxon times. The men wore thick trousers and tunics, with leather shoes. Drawing by Michael Fairley

At this time, Milton Regis was a Royal Estate and one of the largest manorial centres in Kent and the manor (including Bobbing) was recorded as having a population of between 8 and 13 people per square mile.

It was also during the latter part of this period that the Kingdom of Kent was divided into lathes and they in turn were divided into hundreds. Bobbing became part of the half lathe of Milton during the late Saxon period. Farming and agriculture continued to grow throughout this period.

By the time the Domesday book was compiled the area of woodland and forests in Kent had been reduced to 28% of the county. Farming was now a key part of the life of the people living in Bobbing – particularly fruit growing and the growing of corn. For many years there was a flour mill in the village at Bobbing Hill. Root crops also grew well on the loamy, arable soil.

Odo Bishop of Bayeu

The arms of Odo, Bishop of Bayeux and Earl of Kent, the largest landowner in the county

By 1067, Odo, Bishop of Bayeux – William the Conqueror's half brother and now Earl of Kent – had been granted substantial holding of land in Kent and in particular the Royal Manor of Milton. Lands around Milton and Bobbing were in turn let to sub-tenants, later becoming a patchwork of small and medium-sized baronies. The great majority of these land holders came from the same region in Northern France as King William and had supported him at the Battle of Hastings. Other land in the Milton and Bobbing area was held by the church, although this tended to be dispersed and fragmented.

Certainly by the 12th century, the Savage family was already very eminent, had Royal patronage and possessed many estates in Kent, including the manor of Bobbing. The manor house at Bobbing Court – home to Ralph de Savage - was a large building, which was adjacent to where the church stands and believed to be on the site of the current village school. It was said to have a 'fine prospect' on every side.

The life of Bobbing now centred on the manor where court was held and where the Savage family lived. The majority of the villagers were peasantry, smallholders and cottages were tied to the manor and had to render service to their lord although frequently tenants held and worked land for several lords. Most were obliged to plough the lord's land as well as their own.

Other villagers would have been involved in selling food, drink and service to the many travellers passing along Watling Street and, in particular, to the growing number of pilgrims travelling the route through Bobbing to visit the shrine of St Thomas Beckett in Canterbury following his violent death in December 1170, as well as English pilgrims traveling to the Continent. It is estimated that by the middle 1300s up to 180,000 individuals were passing along Watling Street each year. This surely would have made some in Bobbing quite wealthy.

Much of the land around Bobbing at this time was arable, some was pasture for the grazing of livestock and that not occupied by settlements was still woodland. Farming and agriculture, particularly for locally grown corn, barley, other cereals and vegetables, were now to be the pattern of life for the people of Bobbing for the next 300 to 400 years.

During the 14th century, many of the peasant families had small acreages of their own land which would be scattered over several plots. Often no more than 15 acres, they were nevertheless able to grow oats and wheat, keep a few sheep and pigs, maybe a cow and a few horses. Every scrap of land was used. Local markets now played a significant role in the development of village economy.

In 1327 a Peter Marchant (Marchaunt) and a John Marchant were taxpayers in Bobbing and there was a street called Marchant

Street. At the same period there were in the neighbourhood William and John de Coleshalle, Robert and John de Cuttenale and William, John and Alan de Holte. These taxpayers took their names from lands in Bobbing and Iwade – and which today still bear the names of Cutnail's Colsall and Holte or Howe.

In documents of the Taxation Assessment of 1334/5 the tax per thousand acres on crops, livestock and other assets was more than £3. The farming area at this time between Rainham and Faversham – which includes Bobbing - had one of the highest density of taxpayers and payments per thousand acres and was said to be one of the richest in England.

However, in 1348 the plague known as the Black Death swept from London across the whole of Kent and much of England, with something like 45% of the population of the county (recorded as around 75,000 in the 1334/5 tax records) suffering an unfortunate death. Indeed, the Poll Tax of 1377 – over 30 years after the Black Death) shows that the population of Kent had still only recovered to 90,000. Such a population loss would undoubtedly have had a major impact on farming in Bobbing – which would take many years to recover. The population of Kent was still only up to 100,000 by 1500, and no more than 140,000 some 300 years later.

In 1381 the area was affected by the Watt Tyler rebellion against the dreaded Poll Tax which had just been raised to three Groats (one shilling or 5p in today's money) for every person over fifteen years old. The rebels marched to Canterbury along Watling Street, Bobbing.

In 1385 the Norwood genealogical roll used in a lawsuit stated:

'In the first place, Sir Stephen de Northwode, Knight, was seized (held) 310 acres of land, 500 acres of marsh in the Isle of Sheppey, and four score and ten acres of marsh with their pertinences in Upcherche, and of other manors, lands and tenements in the county of Kent.'

Rental documents dated 1404 indicate that the rental of the manor of Northwood Chestnuts (described as Northwode Chasteneys), with land in Milton Regis, Bobbing, Iwade and Lower Halstow was paid with money, cocks, hens and eggs. This manor and land had been part of the Royal Manor of Milton, inherited from the Kings of Kent 500 years earlier, and was carved out of the King's chestnut woods south west of Milton village. As this manor was to be held directly from the royal family, it was made part of Milton, even though Bobbing parish would have physically separated it from Milton.

Local men again took part in a rebellion in 1450. Known as the Cade rebellion some 20,000 Kentish men assembled on Blackheath on the 1st June under the command of Jack Cade of Ashford to protest about the Cinque Ports being exempt from various taxes. There were also rumours that Kent was to be turned into a Royal Deer Forest.

By 1533, one Richard Harris, who was fruiterer to Henry VIII, had purchased land at Teynham and planted England's first apple and cherry trees in Kent. These were imported from southern Europe. The mild climate and fertile soils of that time provided a rich environment for gardens and orchards alike. From this stemmed the garden of England, a great plantation of fruit on the rich brick earthlands. Apple and cherry orchards soon spread from Teynham into the surrounding country and to the lands around Bobbing, turning them from arable land into fruit orchards.

Evidence of how cherry trees had spread to Bobbing by the late 1500s comes from the Kent Quarter Sessions where a Thomas Gray of Bobbing, labourer, and Thomas Clemant of Bobbing, also a labourer, broke into and entered a close owned by William Tayler of Houtehill, Bobbing, and dug up and carried away 35 cherry trees. They were sent to prison.

Up until this time, with the exception of the Roman Road of Watling Street, local roads would have been narrow and twisting unsurfaced byways, tracks or paths used by the villagers, traders and farmers. As agriculture developed farmers would often use the byways to take their cattle or other animals to local ponds or rivers to drink.

In order to stop them wandering off the farmer would interweave hedgerows to form an enclosed pathway to the drinking water or to the market place. Indeed, up until 1555 roads had been the responsibility of the landowners whose property adjoined the road, with bequest sometimes made in a will towards their repair – although this was rare in these parts of the county.

In 1555 an Act was passed making each parish responsible for its roads with surveyors appointed by churchwardens to supervise the work – which was carried out on four selected days each year when every householder either had to assist with repairs or send someone in his place. In 1563 this was increased to six days.

The position of a parish such as Bobbing with the important

national routes along Watling Street and from Maidstone to Sheppey was therefore somewhat dire – particularly as traffic had the right to divert through any unenclosed land adjoining the highway.

By the end of the seventeenth century rates could be levied and labourers hired to do the work more effectively than the reluctant householders. Even then, roads within the parish (with the exception of Watling Street and the Sheppey Way) would still have been tracks full of potholes, rutted and muddy.

It was from the deplorable condition of many roads that turnpiking was enabled through an Act or Parliament which enabled turnpike trusts and private companies to close main roads, construct and maintain a road and charge a toll on those that used the road. Watling Street from Chatham to Canterbury became a turnpike road in 1730 and the Maidstone to Sheppey Road in 1769. A by-product of these toll roads was the provision of milestones, which were made a legal requirement.

Despite the planting of many orchards in Bobbing during the later part of the 1500s, sheep in the 1600s and 1700s were still important in the village. Quarter Sessions records of July 1610 report on the examination of a John Smyth, labourer, regarding sheep brought to a Thomas Goodwin of Bobbing. In the same Quarter Sessions John Smith, labourer at Bobbing, was found not guilty of stealing one lamb worth six shillings and sixpence.

As for the value of a small farm or smallholding estate in the early 1600s, this can be seen from records in 1618 of a Ralph Cranmer of Bobbing. At this time his personal estate was given as

£26.15s.8d, made up of five acres of beans (£3.6s.8d), two-and-a-half acres of wheat already sown (£4), four seams of barley on store (£3), two milch cows (£6) and two hogs (10s) – but no sheep. Ralph Cranmer is shown as having a hall for both living and cooking, probably open to the roof, a buttery at one end and at the other a chamber covered by a loft.

It was around this period of the 1600s that the plague came to the area. Bobbing Parish registers for 1606 and 1609 show that the number of deaths doubled while the number of deaths from the plague in Bobbing was again well above average in 1666 and 1667. This followed the Great Plague, the outbreak of bubonic plague that was particularly violent in London during the hot months of August and September 1665. In one week, 7,165 people died of the plague. The epidemic devastated London and the south east of England with around 70,000 people dying in total – many of them buried in mass graves – and obviously had an impact on the farming community.

In 1642 war broke out between Charles I and Parliament, somewhat interrupting the peace of farming in Bobbing. Kent at this time was immediately secured for Parliament causing many Royalists to leave the county at the start of the ensuing Civil War. Royalist families were liable to have their homes raided and their possessions seized. Leaving Bobbing at this time was a Ralph Clarke of Key Street.

In 1649 the King was executed and in 1655 the Cromwellian Commissioners for Kent were kept busy calling in the King's supporters to give details of their estates – these included Captain

Clarke of Key Street who travelled to London in 1656.

Around the same period, in December 1652, court records show depositions from a John Terry of Bobbing, labourer, who purchased 15 wethers (castrated male sheep) and 2 rams from a Thomas Soames, which were later claimed by two men from East Kent and taken away. Soames claimed that he sold the sheep to Terry on behalf of Richard Browning of Essex.

Farming at this time was not without its other pastimes. Quarter Sessions records of 1598 indicate that Alexander Bailye of Bobbing, a husbandman – the name for a farmer of that time – appeared to answer questions regarding the begetting of a bastard child to Isabel Willares of Bobbing, a spinster of the parish. Isabel presented information concerning the child and about Alexander, the reputed father.

Similar records for 1596 are for a court order regarding Isabel Cockes of Bobbing and a John Haies of Milton for the maintenance of Godfrey, their bastard child. Rather later, in 1699, a court deposition was presented by an Elizabeth Brooman of Bobbing that John Lushington of Rainham, a victualler, was the father of her bastard child.

Perhaps some of this begetting of children came from too much alcohol. At the Kent Quarter Sessions in September 1601 John Wade of Bobbing, a victualler, was charged that from 30th May 1598 to the 20th July 1601, he kept at Bobbing, "A common tiplinge howse" and sold "Ale and Beere" without a licence. It was recorded that he did not turn up and a writ ordering his arrest was issued so that he would appear at the next session.

By medieval times the area was so important that an annual 'fayre' was held on land close to where Bobbing Village Hall stands today. This 'fayre' was said to be the equal of the great Nottingham fayre – one of the largest in England. Deeds of 1690 also showed a 'spittle house in Key Street in Bobbing and the right of patronage thereto.'

It was from this period that many of the farmhouses in the manor of Bobbing started to be built. Much of the area to the north

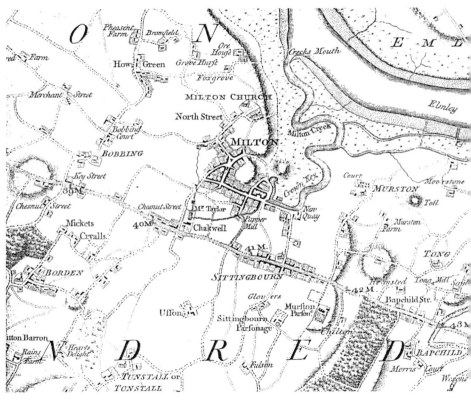

Detail from a topographical map of the Sittingbourne, Milton and Bobbing are 1769. Bobbing Court, Pheasent Farm, Norwood Farm (Norred), How Green, Street and Merchant Street are all indicated

west of what is now the main A249 road through Bobbing was rural farmland with scattered farms and outbuilding. Great Norwood Barn dates back to the 17th century; Great Norwood Farmhouse in Parsonage Lane to the sixteenth century. The original farmhouse on this site was a fortified manor house used as a hunting lodge by King John and King Stephen. It is known that this house burnt down and from the remnants of this property the existing farmhouse was built. An early chapel is believed to have been within the original moated site.

The White House and Uppertoes and Nethertoes, which are along the old Sheppey Way, are also 16th century buildings. Church Farm Cottages – originally a 15th century Hall house – was a later conversion to farm cottages. Pheasants Farmhouse was built around 1700; Sole Place in 1702. These old building are undoubtedly some of the most architecturally interesting in the village. Bobbing Place is a later build from the 19th century, although the walled garden around it is from the 17th century.

Many of these traditional local buildings are likely to be timber framed with a lower roof of red brick and upper floor lined with weather boards. The roof would be of hand-made Kent peg roof tiles. Buildings constructed in this way are likely to be 'listed'. Bricks made from local clay are yellow and there a number of local houses made from these. The use of flints is another traditional local building material – as seen with Bobbing School and the Church.

Because of local shipbuilding at Milton, Sheernes and Queenborough, old ships timbers were often used for the timber framed buildings. Windows were usually multi-paned, often with eight panes with the main frame, or more if leaded. Doors were made of solid wood.

It was during the period from the middle 1500s to the end of the 1700s that the North Kent region - which included Bobbing- was said to be one of the most vibrant and commercial farming areas of England. There was a windmill at Bobbing Hill for grinding flour and the area was well placed for the transporting of food to London through the port of Milton. Many farmers would have been growing rich. So much so, that the Land Tax for the Sittingbourne and Faversham districts was between 20 pence and 40 pence per acre for much of the 1700s – one of the highest in the county.

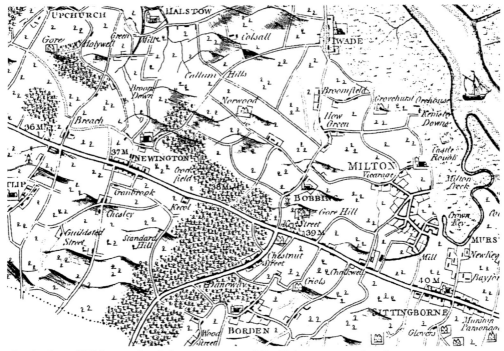

In the late 1700s much of the area around Bobbing was orchards

It can be seen that, throughout the history of Bobbing, that its main economic activity was agriculture and farming, predominately fruit farming from the mid 1500s to the 1900s. A map of the late 1700s shows much of the Bobbing area as orchards. Bobbing Court, the manorial centre of the village, and many of the small farms were passed down through the generations from father to son. The actual methods of farming throughout this time changed very little and were largely labour intensive.

Many of the farms that were established in the 16th to 18th centuries had tied cottages attached to them or at least close by. Church and census records for Bobbing over the years show that many generations of the same family worked on the farms. Many of the farms would have employed fifty or more men and, at busy harvest or fruit picking times, many more. Farming contributed enormously to Kent's economy throughout this time.

Some of the names recorded as living and working in Bobbing during the 17th century include Chris Kennard, Fran Reynolds (vicar of Bobbing), John Reader (another vicar of Bobbing), William Plott Snr, Thomas Miller, Anne Meade, Rich Merriam, John Rayner (Bobbing farm), Phillis Tong, Hy Pannell, Ellis Hatch, Geo Wynne, Rich Lees, Thomas Turner (curate of Bobbing), John Turner, victualler and Rich Pidgeon, a yeoman.

In 1801, the Tithe award schedule for Bobbing showed land acreage of 1,068 and a population in the village of 231 people. By 1901 the population had risen to 555. Landowners listed in the Tithe schedules during this period included Sir John Maxwell Tylden, the Earl of Aylesford, Sir Richard Powlett Geary, the Rev.

George Simpson and Baroness Sophia Elizabeth Wenman.

Various documents from the 1700 to 1800s show how land changed hands and sometimes its value. The release of a lease in July 1722 between Robert Brake of Rochester and Francis Brooke of Town Malling and Thomas Crofford of London and Philip Brooke, of some 300 acres in the Manor of Northwood in the parishes of Milton, Lower Halstow, Bobbing, Newington and Iwade took place for a consideration of £500.

Nethertoes, formerly the estate of the Barrows family, was given by William Barrow in 1707 amongst other estates in Kent, for the benefit of the poor of Borden. Various deeds between 1796 and 1898 refer to 340 acres of land at Bobbing; an 1898 deed and map with valuations, estimates, sale notices and inventories relating to a Bobbing Court Farm and a lease for 1 acre of land adjoining Gorehill in Bobbing.

Various leases and settlements issued during the 1700s relate to the Sole family of Bobbing Place. There are records of leases to Thomas Sole, the shipbuilder, in 1718; to Cockin Sole in 1726 – this was for the lease of Milton Regis rectory for an annual payment of £21 12s 6d and of 5 quarters of wheat and 10 quarters of barley in kind or in money. Sole was to also pay the vicar of Milton a specified pension.

The arms of the Sole family of Bobbing.

In 1750 John Cockin Sole put leasehold properties in Bobbing in trust for the children of John Cockin Sole and, in 1784, there is a record of the marriage settlement on the engagement of John Cockin Sole and Catherine Lushington between Sole and Thomas Godfrey Lushington, Catherine's father. John Cockin Sole, said to be a descendent of the Lords of the Manor of Soles, was the High Sheriff of Kent in 1756.

In 1810, a copy of a marriage settlement between Sir William Geary and Henrietta Dering (born Henrietta Nevil in County Kildare, Ireland), widow of Sir Edward Deering included 63 acres in Bobbing and Milton-next-Sittingbourne; 60 acres in the Manor of Upper Toes and 60 acres in Milton-next-Sittingbourne, Iwade and Bobbing. At this time Sir William Geary of Oxenhoath was already one of the major land holders in the area.

Sir William Geary was an MP for Kent between 1796 and 1806 and again from 1812 to 1818. He was the son of Admiral Sir Francis Geary who for a time commanded the Channel Fleet during a critical period of the threatened French Invasion of England. Sir Francis Geary was also said to be the main mentor to Nelson, who went on to win the Battle of Trafalgar.

In 1812, a freehold and leasehold estate comprising manor and farm with 1,000 acres in Upchurch, Newington, Lower Halstow, Bobbing, Hartlip and Detling was auctioned at the Crown Inn, Rochester. The consideration is not mentioned.

However, not everything was well. In a petition of inhabitants of many of the villages in Kent – including Bobbing - in 1830, the petitioners said that they were experiencing great difficulty in bearing the weight of taxation with the diminished prices of agricultural produce and asked Parliament for full relief from existing oppressive taxes on malt and beer.

Wages for farm servants in the early 1800s averaged less than 5/- (25p) a week; £12 a year for a trained man, while boys received 4d (1½p) a week. Winter wages for an expert farm worker were around 5s (25p). In comparison, the cost of a horse-drawn coach journey to London was £1.4s.0d (£1.20p) inside the coach and 18.0s outside.

Little wonder that there was further unrest in the county with the so-called 'Swing riots' of 1830. They were known as the 'Swing riots' because of threatening letters signed by a 'Captain Swing' being received by some farmers. This was not an organized plot just some spontaneous outbreaks of lawlessness by poor farm labourers. Their grievances included low wages, unemployment, poor living conditions, and the growing use of threshing machines. Machines from the industrial revolution were taking away their livelihood and their lifestyle had been reduced to subsistence level.

In October 1830, with the county of Kent being in turmoil, Thomas Knight of Bobbing was unpopular enough to have his farm chosen as a target for one of these riotous attacks. Machinery and property were severely damaged and he was fortunate to get away with his life.

Fortunately the revolt died away in 1831 after savage sentences were passed on those found guilty. However, the conditions of farm labourers remained largely unchanged.

These issues, together with taxation and price pressures on the tenant farmers meant that by around 1859 there were said to be few local smallholders in the area who were left farming with less than

10 acres of land; economic circumstances and new machinery had forced them out of business.

Nevertheless, place names on the Bobbing Ordnance Survey map of 1905 still included land at Cambray Farm, Coldharbour, Howt Green, Pigeon Farm, Toes, Upper and Nether and Webbend Ditch.

Towards the end of the 1800s there was a further recession in Kent farming. Bad seasons, frosts, heavy snow, late springs, all contributed to this recessionary period. In January 1867 for example, heavy snows and snowdrifts in Kent of up to 6 feet in depth blocked roads and railways as well as causing damage to fruit trees. More heavy snow at the end of January that year wrecked overhead telegraph lines and again wrecked trees. Up to two foot of snow was reported.

Heavy snow falls in Kent in November 1890 – with up to two foot of snow, again damaged trees. But this was nothing compared with the winter of 1894/5 when air frosts down to -3 degrees Centigrade occurred for 70 out of the 84 nights between 26th December and 20th March. For part of this time the whole of the Thames was more or less blocked by ice floes of some 6 to 7ft in thickness. Even water mains were frozen below the surface down to depths of just under three feet. Heavy snow was also experienced during this period.

Such were the problems of the weather and the farming depression in the late 1800s that farmers took acres of farm land out of cultivation just in order to survive. Indeed, in *Bobbing in 1881* by HD Allinson, it is stated that 'most of the men in the parish were farmworkers and that they worked at that time for only four farmers in Bobbing. Of the four farmers, Mr R Knight farmed by far the largest acreage and lived at Bobbing Court which he rented with the land from Rev Simpson.'

This Bobbing Court was the manor house of the village, although not the same one as which had been the former home of the Savage and Clifford families. This earlier property had been pulled down in the eighteenth century and a new one built on the foundations of the old one.

Allinson also wrote that 'in 1881, 25 of the men of Bobbing and 8 boys were employed by Mr Knight to farm the 950 acres.' These boys would have started work on the farm at the age of 13 after leaving Bobbing School.

'Of the four farmers in Bobbing' stated Allinson 'only E Hamet owned the land he farmed and this amounted to 137 acres in the Howt Green area, his farm was Stickfast Farm – later called Cambray Farm, Stickfast Lane. At Nethertoes Farm, Howt Green, William Foord farmed 94 acres and employed only 2 men and 1 boy. His land was rented from the Trustees of the Estate of William Barrow of Borden who died in 1707 leaving large estates, the income of which was to be used for the benefit of the poor.'

The only other farmer in Bobbing at this time was William Luckhurst, who rented Chestnut Farm from the Rev George Simpson. This 36 acre farm employed 4 men and 3 boys. There was also some market gardening in Bobbing at this time, while there was still a working windmill producing flour at Bobbing Hill. This windmill is shown on local maps of Bobbing as far back as 1769, but was pulled down in 1902. Two blacksmiths, a wheelwright and carpenters were also to be found in the village in 1881.

Farms with land shown in the Parish Register of 1897 included Quinton Farm (Robert Cornford), Chestnut Street Farm (John Greensted), Cutnails Farm (John Hinge), Nethertoes Farm (Edward Maxted), Uppertoes Farm (James Stevens) and Church Farm (Albert Ernest Wood).

Although the main crops grown in Bobbing in the 1890s were oats, wheat, barley, hops and fruit orchards it is noted that one hundred years later by the 1990s, most of the orchards of Bobbing had been grubbed out following the demise of fruit farming. The cherries, plums, apples and pears that first started coming to the village in the 1500s were now largely gone to be

Rosemount Kentish Smock Mill at Bobbing Hill. Demolished in 1902. Drawing by Peter Judges

replaced by huge fields of arable crops or livestock grazing – very much back to the days before fruit growing came to Bobbing, although now with a much larger area of unbroken fields. It is also recorded in the Sittingbourne, Milton & District Directory of 1908 that a few acres of hops were also grown in Bobbing parish, together with some root crops.

One of the most prominent farmers in Bobbing during much of the 1900s, Jim Mackleden, died in 1999. A well-respected mixed farmer with 2,000 acres around Swale, he specialised in livestock.

Mr Mackleden was born and lived – apart from being evacuated to Wales during the war years – at Bobbing Court. His expertise in livestock was rewarded by prizes at many shows. He was also a steadfast supporter of the Young Farmers Club at Westlands School

With the demise of farming many of the old farm cottages and farm buildings were sold, often to house small local businesses. What farmland was left was able to be run by just a few men using more intensive farming techniques.

The great days of farming and agriculture in and around Bobbing were now largely gone.

A time of progress and change

The 1800s and early 1900s were a period of great change for the towns and villages of Kent, with many new Acts of Parliament starting to have an effect on the welfare and social life of people at a national, district and local level. Improvements in public health, water supply, hospital provisions and sewerage were all introduced; fire and ambulance services came into being; gas and electricity started to be supplied; trains and the telegraph were introduced as well as advances in education and the establishment of libraries.

In the early 18th C for example, the supply of water to towns and villages in Kent was often rudimentary. Water tended to be drawn from rivers and springs and supplied through public tanks and wells or through conduits and the use of water carts. These methods of water supply meant that the people of Kent suffered from regular attacks of infectious diseases – such as measles, whooping cough and cholera. Indeed, it is recorded that there were regular outbreaks of cholera around Sittingbourne, Milton and Bobbing between the years of 1830 and 1866.

Hospital provision for those with infectious disease were either inadequate or non-existent at this time and death from cholera and other diseases of the time would often be the consequence.

The provision of clean water, the removal of sewage and improved hospital facilities for infectious diseases were therefore seen as the key to eliminating the problem and the Government began to introduce Public Health Acts of Parliament from this time. Schemes to improve water supply were also promoted by Acts of

Parliament and from around 1850 most towns and villages began to establish waterworks and offer a clean supply of water with freedom from contamination or infection. Such was the case with the water supply for Sittingbourne, Milton and the villages of Bobbing, Bredgar, Borden, etc.

A water supply for Sittingbourne and the surrounding district was established in the 1860s and this belonged to the town. The Works for this were situated at Keycol Hill, one of the highest points in Bobbing. The original site for this Waterworks was purchased on Feb 15th, 1868. This occupied two rods (11 yards). On Oct 23rd 1895 the purchase of another 1 1/2 acres was completed and the Works were further extended

According to Bobbing Parish records of March 1896 work was commencing that month for the laying on of water for the Parish. A request was put forward at that time for the erection of a stand pipe at Web End Ditch corner and also for fire hydrants to be placed near Bobbing Church and School in case there was fire

There were two reservoirs at the Waterworks, with a capacity of 300,000 and 147,000 gallons respectively. The boring extended 420 feet below the surface. The pumping of the water from the bore holes to the reservoirs was by steam power and two boilers were installed. The Works and wells were subsequently lit by electricity. By the early 1900s Deacon Water Waste Detecting Meters had also been installed in various parts of the town

A few years on – in 1880 – from the establishment in Bobbing of a clean water supply for the district the Sittingbourne and Milton Joint Hospital Board was formed, and a Hospital

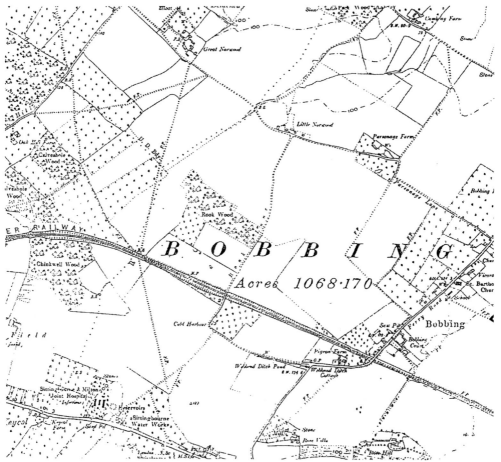

Detail based on a map of 1865 showing the main Canterbury to London Railway line passing through Bobbing and the Sittingbourne Waterworks and Isolation hospital at Keycol

and Sanatorium for the treatment of cases of infectious disease in the area was built at Keycol Hill, Bobbing, in 1887 at a cost of about £5,000. The Hospital was enlarged from time to time and, by the early 1900s was a thoroughly modern institution capable of accommodating up to 100 patients. It was shut down in 1998 and demolished in 2004 for the building of housing.

About the same time the district Workhouse, a large and rambling series of buildings built in 1835 for 350 inmates and which was situated in North Street Milton, was significantly extended to include a modern infirmary for people of the district, again including Bobbing. A Medical Officer for the District was appointed in 1905.

Other new services were being introduced to Sittingbourne and the surrounding villages in the later part of the 1800s. A Sittingbourne and District Fire Brigade - a volunteer brigade supported by public donation - was formed in 1874. This was re-organised in 1897 with a Mr. Hedley Peters taking the command. The same year a fine steam fire engine was acquired by public subscription, and new premises for the Brigade were opened in Crescent Street, Sittingbourne. Later a fire escape was obtained.

In Bobbing Parish Council records of August 1897 a letter was read from the Sittingbourne Urban Council stating that for the use of their fire engine to fight fires in the Parish of Bobbing there would an annual charge of $4.10s.0d.

But then the Brigade was said to be 'assiduously drilled and to be second to no other Brigade in the county, winning honours in both the South Eastern Counties and All England competitions under the National Fire Brigades' Union. In the early 1900s the Brigade won the steam fire engine championship of the South-Eastern Counties three times. It also won the hose cart and ambulance championships on several occasions.'

Again in the late 1800s the Brickmasters of the district

subscribed and presented to the town a three-stretcher horse ambulance This was housed and operated from the Fire Brigade premises in Crescent Street. The ambulance was available in cases of accident for any parish in the Milton Union – including Bobbing. It was available for any operation case. In operation cases horse-hire had to be paid for - except in necessitous cases - when a fund (provided for the purpose) was available to be drawn upon.

Following the successful demonstration of Stephenson's 'Rocket' in 1829, railways were soon to extend into Kent. Indeed, the first steam-hauled, public railway in Southern England was opened between Canterbury and Whitstable in 1830, followed six years later by the London and Greenwich Railway. An Act of Parliament in 1836 saw the first major railway in Kent linking London to Dover, via Ashford. The main railway line built by the London, Chatham and Dover Railway (LCDR) company came through Bobbing in 1858, while a branch line running to the Isle of Sheppey was added around one year later. At that time the cost for passengers was said to be one pence per mile (which was actually quite expensive for the time). While other lines in Kent struggled to be profitable, the LCDR was fortunate to gain a contract for the transport of continental mail from Dover to London in 1861 thus ensuring the line's ongoing success and growth.

Reference to the railway can be seen in a Parish Council record of June 1902 when it was directed that a letter be sent to the railway company asking for gates to be replaced at the crossing leading to the Grove rather than the public having to use the stile that had been erected there instead of the gates.

The gates were replaced in November 1902.

With the growth of the railways in Kent came the development of the telegraph, enabling telephones to be introduced into places such as Bobbing from around the 1880s onwards. Even before that, maps of 1865 and 1869 show an 'electric telegraph' along the Sheppey Way and, again, an electric telegraph and a Post Office that was in existence half way up Keycol Hill.

Other key developments to improve the life of the inhabitants of Bobbing were also being introduced in the 1800s. Great improvements in the manufacture and use of gas for lighting and cooking came to the village after the 1860s as gas mantles were introduced for the lighting of the street and homes, while gas for cooking started to be introduced after the 1870s.

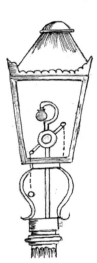

Gas lamps along Key Street were lit each day by a man that came round on a bicycle. He had a long rod with a chain on the end. A hook on the end of the chain would click on to the tip of the lamp, which would then bring on the light.

Education was a further advance. The Elementary Education Act of 1870 set the framework for schooling for all children between the ages of 5 and 13. This Act enabled School Boards to be established which could raise funds from a rate, build and run schools, subsidise church schools, pay the fees of the poorest children and could impose a by-law making attendance compulsory.

The one/only gas light in Key Street opposite the Wesleyan Chapel 1897 - 1962. Drawing by Peter Judges

Between 1870 and 1880, almost 4000 schools were started or taken over by school boards, including Bobbing Church of England Primary School. The original foundation stone for the School was laid in 1865 and the building completed in 1869. This stone can still be seen inside the reception area of the (recently enlarged) school. It was built on the site of the original Bobbing Court that was pulled down in 1748.

1

The very first entry in the Bobbing School logbook in March 1872. Illustration courtesy of Bobbing School

The school was placed under Government control on March 10th 1872, the headmistress at that time being Miss Wilmot Watson. It was enlarged in 1882 to accommodate 120 children, further enlarged in 1908 – when 'several commodious classrooms were added' - and enlarged again in 2001 to cater for 220 children. Average attendance in 1881 was 66 pupils.

Between 1895 and 1931 – a total of 36 years - the school was run by the only head master that was ever appointed, Mr Skinner. He was followed by Miss Whelan as head mistress who was at the school for a further 34 years. Education however, was not new to the village even in the 1870s. A Church of England School is recorded in Canterbury Diocese records as being in the village from 1540 to 1835.

These individual School Boards were abolished by the Education Act of 1902, which replaced them with Local Education Authorities and extended their remit to include secondary education for the very first time.

Apart from Bobbing Church of England School there was also a private school in a large house on Bobbing Hill opposite the Key Inn at Key Street. In this residential school lived borders from as far away as France. It was run by a Mr Samuel Mobbs from Northamptonshire with his wife and son Edgar. All three taught the boys and girls who numbered 18 in 1881. Their ages ranged from 10 to 19 years. Three of the pupils came from France and there were four servants to cook and clean the house.

In June 1975 another school was opened at Grove Park with a capacity for 300 children. This was a modern single storey building in a square format. On one side the school ground stretched into the country, on the other side was the Grove Park Estate. The head teacher at this time was Mr O Waters and there were eight other teachers, a secretary, class helpers and kitchen staff.

Another Government Act which was to have implications for Bobbing was the Local Government Act of 1894 which divided the rural areas of England into some 14,000 parishes. Although these new parishes largely followed the traditional parish boundaries that had been formed by 1200 the Act removed or detached various anomalies and enabled parish affairs to be controlled by an elected parish council.

Following the introduction of the Act, Bobbing Parish Council was established in 1895. Bobbing Council currently consists of nine voluntary Councillors who are elected for a four-year term of office to care for the parish and serve and administer the needs of the residents. The Council employs a part time

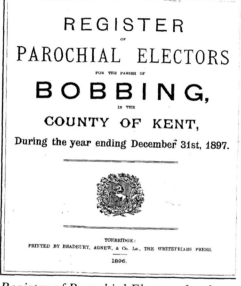

REGISTER
of
PAROCHIAL ELECTORS
FOR THE PARISH OF
BOBBING,
IN THE
COUNTY OF KENT,
During the year ending December 31st, 1897.

TONBRIDGE:
PRINTED BY BRADBURY, AGNEW, & Co. Ld., THE WHITEFRIARS PRESS.
1896.

Register of Parochial Electors for the Parish of Bobbing, December 31st, 1897.

Parish Clerk who acts as a focal point and to implement council decisions.

Bobbing Parish Council meetings are usually held on the first Wednesday of every month in the Village Hall and are open to the public. Any elector wishing the council to discuss an issue needs to tell the Parish Clerk at least three clear days before the day of the meeting. The Parish Council also holds an Annual Parish Meeting where all electors in the Parish can attend an annual review of Parish events and organisations.

At this time, in the early 1900s, the Milton Union comprised a total of eighteen parishes, which together totalled some 32,546 acres in extent, and had a population of about 29,000. The parishes included at this time were Bapchild, Bobbing, Borden, Bredgar, Halstow, Hartlip, Iwade Kingsdown, Milsted, Milton, Murston, Newington, Rainham, Rodmersham, Sittingbourne, Tong, Tunstall, and Upchurch. The total rateable value for all the parishes was £144,637. The member of the Board of Guardians for Bobbing at this time was a W F Drake.

By 1911, public libraries were being introduced for the benefit of the town and parishes of Sittingbourne, with the public swimming bath in the town being built in 1913.

When war broke out in 1914 recruiting rallies were held everywhere; there were also appeals for recruiting agents in the local press and one such agent was appointed for every village. Special constables were sworn in to keep watch over the parish at this time. Bombs were dropped on nearby Borden on April 16th 1915 by an aeroplane that had already dropped bombs on Faversham. Zeppelins were also seen flying overhead on their way to London.

Apart from the railways, bus services were also now part of the way of life for Bobbing residents, although Parish records for

Key Street in 1900. Picture courtesy of Sittingbourne Heritage Museum.

The Sanatorium, Keycol Hill Hospital, in the early 1900s. Picture courtesy of Sittingbourne Heritage Museum

plate 3

Bobbing Football Team of 1911/912. Picture courtesy of Sittingbourne Heritage Museum

Mackelden farm workers in the 1930s. Photo courtesy of Peter Judges.

plate 4

Headmistress of Bobbing School, Miss J M Whelan, photographed with the senior class in 1946

Teacher Mrs Seed with a school class from Bobbing School in 1949

plate 5

Laying of the Foundation Stone of Bobbing Village Hall in 1953 by farmer Mr Ernie Mackelden and Mr Percy Wells, MP. Photo courtesy of Peter Judges.

Bobbing Conservative's Christmas Party in December 1953.
Photo courtesy of Peter Judges.

plate 6

December 1927 show that the Council decided to point out to Maidstone & District Motor Services that the fare of threepence (3d) from Key Street to Sittingbourne was excessive and that the Council suggested this be reduced to twopence (2d).

The George Andrews Fountain erected for the opening of Gore Court Cricket grounds in 1937 - pulled down by Swale Council in 1980. Drawing by Peter Judges.

In 1937 George Andrews, the Managing Director of the brickfields at Murston, together with his son Harold, Chairman of both the Gore Court Hockey and Cricket Clubs, fixed a deal for a piece of land known as the Grove near Key Street and was canny enough to invest the ownership of the lands in the hands of the Council, provided the centre portion was leased for Gore Court Cricket Club for a period of 399 years. Before that, William Thomson grazed his dairy cows on the land.

Bobbing can also lay claim in that it is said to be the home of the first ever set of traffic lights to be installed in Kent in 1937. This was just prior to World War II when traffic at Key Street crossroads was so bad as to warrant the purchase and installation of a set of traffic lights to control the traffic flow across the junction. What a legacy for a small village to leave to the county.

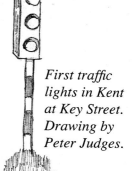

First traffic lights in Kent at Key Street. Drawing by Peter Judges.

In 1946 regulars at the Halfway House public

house in Bobbing suggested a cricket team. The Landlord of the pub, Jack Wibley, was an ex professional footballer for Crystal Palace and a talented cricketer. Early members of this Bobbing Cricket Club were Jack Wibley, Jack Bisham, George Bruce and George Weely and the first game was an evening fixture against Iwade, at Iwade, on Thursday 6th June 1946. Bobbing won by 20 runs.

At the end of 1946 Dick Bensted gave the Club a small meadow behind Pheasants garage. Later Jim Mackleden and his father Ernie Mackleden gave a suitably sized meadow in Rook Lane and, in 1948, this ground was christened the Halfway Oval. The tea hut was a khaki tent just inside the gate.

The first pavilion was an RAF barrack hut from Detling aerodrome. However, its life was short lived as it was destroyed by fire a few years later. The Club's annual subs were increased in 1957 to £1.0.5. The cost of teas was increased to 2/6d (12½p) and the match fee to one shilling (5p). Details taken from the Bobbing Court Book 1946-1984.

In the mid 1960s a residential housing estate containing a parade of shops and a primary school was built at Grove Park. Bobbing Village Hall was started in 1953 with the foundation stone being laid by Mr Mackleden and Percy Wells, the local MP. Bobbing residents raised £2,000 towards the cost of the Hall. This sum purchased 61,000 bricks and, with voluntary labour over a period of three weeks, these were moved and stacked ready for when building work started.

By 1980 the crossroads at Key Street had become infamous for traffic delays and further highway improvements were necessary. So much so that it was decided to demolish most of the community of Key Street, including the public house, garage, shops and various residential homes to make way for a road improvement scheme incorporating a roundabout and a new road alignment.

However, by 1995 even this road improvement had proved to be inadequate and another major road improvement scheme was implemented to incorporate a multi-level interchange being built to carry a new duel carriageway Maidstone to Sheppey Road (the A249) underneath the old Key Street 'Watling Street' Road. This involved demolishing even more of the former Key Street community.

Having survived over two thousand years of history the Roman Road through Bobbing still lives on, but the community the road spawned has largely disappeared. Over a 15 year period from the early 1980s something like 50 buildings, including the public house, private school, residential homes, shops and a chapel, were all demolished to make way for road improvements.

Then, in 1996, Swale Council approved a planning application for 230 houses at The Meads, Bobbing. This was the first phase of the draft Swale Local Plan which would see land made available on a site bounded by rail lines to the south and east, the new A249 to the west and Quinton Road to the north for up to 750 homes, offices and business development, shops, a primary school and a community woodland. Such is progress.

By 1998 Bobbing Parish Council were claiming that the village was in danger of being wiped out because of all the major road developments, the loss of 50 buildings, the development of The Meads almost as a village in its own right, the loss of village identity and increased traffic.

Certainly a disappointing end to the 20th century in which the village of Bobbing was not treated well. Increasingly heavy traffic, a major through route, in turn wrapped around with new roads and plans for hundreds of new homes, have made Bobbing pretty well indistinguishable from its historic past.

The Battle over Bobbing

In July 1940, during the early part of World War II, the German airforce attempted to gain superiority over the Royal Air Force before they could begin a planned air and sea invasion of Britain. The aim was to attack RAF airfields and aircraft production centres, as well as terrorizing the British people into submission.

So began the most intense period of daylight air raiding which went on for four months. This period was known as the Battle of Britain and was the first major battle to be fought entirely in the air. Most of this battle was over southern England with German bombers and fighters coming over and then being engaged in combat by the RAF.

Villagers in Bobbing, as with other towns and villages, were given a wide variety of leaflets at this time. One of these, 'War Emergency – Information and Instructions' set out instructions for the public, including what to do when there was an Air Raid Warning, the carrying of identity labels and the sewing of name labels into children's clothing, Fire Precautions, instructions to drivers of vehicles and cyclists, closure of schools, evacuation of children, organization

WAR EMERGENCY

INFORMATION AND
INSTRUCTIONS

Read this leaflet carefully and make sure that you and all other responsible persons in your house understand its contents.

Pay no attention to rumours. Official news will be given in the papers and over the wireless.

Listen carefully to all broadcast instructions and be ready to note them down.

War Emergency leaflet issued to all Bobbing households at the beginning of the War

of food supplies, and the payment of pensions and allowances.

Another leaflet issued to villagers by Kent County Constabulary urged the population to 'stay put' in the event of invasion by the Germans as well as when sirens sounded, when bombs were exploding or when anti-aircraft guns were firing. The leaflet explained that the enemy had been known to fire machine guns to bring people out to watch and then to drop bombs on them. An official German message which had been captured said 'Watch for civilian refugees on the roads. Harass them as much as possible.'

'Stay Where You are' if invaded instructions to the people of Bobbing

This information was important as near to Bobbing was an Anti-Aircraft Battery at Chetney, just the other side of Iwade. Apart from the Ack Ack guns there were searchlights and barrage balloons. During this period of war the sound of guns firing at German sorties as well as aircraft dog fights overhead became a regular part of village life. The barrage balloons could be easily seen from Bobbing and, at night, searchlights would criss-cross the sky.

At one stage householders in Bobbing were intrigued to find their gardens strewn with pieces of paper, some were black stripes silvered on one side and others were black on both side with a silver lining. The discoveries coincided with enemy planes passing over the village. These pieces of paper were droppedb y the German planes and designed to nullify the effect of British radio-location equipment and render it less accurate.

Houses in the village were told to black-out all windows, skylights, glazed doors or other openings which would show a light at night and to screen these with dark blinds, curtains, blankets or brown paper so that no light would be visible outside at night. All lighted signs and advertisements and other outside lights had to be turned off.

Similarly, villagers were not allowed to drive or cycle at night unless their lights were dimmed and screened. Cars also had to be used sparingly as the supply of petrol was rationed while telephones were only to be used for very urgent messages.

Other documents issued to villagers explained what to do 'If the Invader comes'. This included advice to keep watch if they saw anything suspicious, note it down and then go at once to the nearest police officer or station – and not to rush about spreading vague rumours. It also gave guidance about hiding food, bicycles and maps, putting cars out of action and making sure that the enemy was not able to get any petrol.

Even early in the war, families were urged to prepare air-raid shelters, or to have a trench ready in their garden. Advice was also available from the local Air Raid Warden which told everyone how to prepare a shelter in their house. Many villagers at this time erected pre-fabricated Anderson air raid shelters in their gardens, or installed indoor shelters (called Morrison shelters) in their houses.

AIR RAID PRECAUTIONS.
Cert. No. 67

Local Authority:—SWALE RURAL DISTRICT COUNCIL.

Local Certificate of Anti=Gas Training.

This is to Certify that Mr N.H.Batt

"Hailey", Key Street, Sittingbourne

has completed a **COURSE OF ANTI-GAS TRAINING** held under the auspices of the Swale Rural District Council and has acquired sufficient knowledge of Anti-Gas measures* to act as indicated in Grade (iii) below

Nature of Course attended Anti-Gas, High Explosive and Incendiary Bomb.

Name and Qualification of Instructor A.E.Walter A.R.P.(Special).

Dated 25th May 1939   **Signed** G.S.Goodwin
                                   On behalf of Local Authority.

(The Conditions governing the award of this Certificate are shown below. This Certificate is to be regarded as of Local Validity only).

Ex^d.   CONDITIONS OF AWARD.

1. The qualifications obtainable on anti-gas courses arranged by the Local Authority are as follows :—
   (i)   Has acquired sufficient knowledge of anti-gas measures for personal protection.
   (ii) Has acquired sufficient knowledge of anti-gas measures to act as a member of a public air raid precautions service.
   (iii) Has acquired sufficient knowledge of anti-gas measures to act as an assistant to an anti-gas instructor (see condition 3).
2. This certificate does not qualify the holder to act as an instructor under any circumstances.
3. If the qualification to act as an assistant to an anti-gas instructor has been endorsed on the certificate, the holder is eligible to assist at anti-gas training courses held by a qualified Instructor engaged in giving instruction on behalf of the Local Authority.

Certificate of Anti-Gas Training awarded by Swale Rural District Council to Mr. N H Batt of Key Street in May 1939

As part of the Air Raid Precautions, Swale Rural District Council instituted courses of anti-gas training and in May 1939 Mr N H Batt of Key Street successfully completed a course on anti-gas, high explosive and incendiary bomb measures for which he received an appropriate certificate. He was appointed an Air Raid Warden on the 25th May. Head Warden for the area was Mr F Mackelden.

At Bobbing school, a re-inforced air-raid shelter was eventually built onto the side of the school next to the church. Whenever air raid sirens sounded the schoolchildren would take refuge in the

I WISH TO MARK, BY THIS PERSONAL MESSAGE, my appreciation of the service you have rendered to your Country in 1939 —

In the early days of the War you opened your door to strangers who were in need of shelter, & offered to share your home with them.

I know that to this unselfish task you have sacrificed much of your own comfort, & that it could not have been achieved without the loyal co-operation of all in your household —

By your sympathy you have earned the gratitude of those to whom you have shown hospitality, & by your readiness to serve you have helped the State in a work of great value —

Elizabeth R

Mrs. Fairley.

Letter sent by Her Majesty Queen Elizabeth to Dorothy Fairley in 1939 to thank her for taking in evacuees from Sussex during the Battle of Britain.

plate 7

Burnt segment of a German pilot's map found next to a Messerschmitt 109 that was shot down in flames over Bobbing in August 1940.

plate 8

shelter and continue with their lessons, often to the background sound of gunfire or bombs exploding.

Fortunately the school was never hit, although it came close on the 24th August 1940 during the early days of the Battle of Britain when a German airplane crashed within a few yards of the school.

The result of a dogfight between a Hawker Hurricane and a Messerschmitt ME109 being flown by Uffz Herbert Müller the German 'plane on its way home after escorting a bombing raid on Hornchurch aerodrome, closely followed by the British aircraft flown by Pilot Officer Kenneth John Marston, was hit by gunfire and, flying ever lower over the cherry orchard stretching between Quinton Lane and Bobbing Church, just avoided Bobbing Church before crashing into scrubland on Mackledens Farm immediately behind Bobbing school.

The German pilot was buried in Bobbing churchyard, only yards from where he had crashed and died. The church was paid £1 a year to look after the grave. In the 1980s Herbert Müller was re-interred in a War Cemetery in Germany. Unfortunately, the British pilot also died just a few weeks after his dogfight with Müller following a mid-air crash.

An idea of the intensity of the air raids and battle over the skies in and around Bobbing at this time can be gained from extracts from the diary of Charles Fairley, Quinton Lane, Bobbing, during a five week period in 1940 during the early part of the Battle of Britain:

26th August	*– Two air raids today*
27th August	*– Two air raids today*
28th August	*– German Messerschmitt crashes by Bobbing Church. Dornier shot down Five air raids during the day*
28th August	*– German Dornier shot down*
29th August	*– Two air raids*
30th August	*– Four air raids*
31st August	*– Four air raids*
1st September	*– Four air raids*
2nd September	*– Two German planes shot down after coming over Sheppey. Two air raids today*
3rd September	*– Four air raids today*
4th September	*– Saw parachute came down over Stockbury area. Four air raids today*
5th September	*– Three air raids*
6th September	*– Four air raids*
7th September	*– Saw German plane shot down and heard another from which we saw parachute descent. Found shrapnel in garden*
8th September	*– Three air raids*
9th September	*– Another German plane shot down over Bobbing. Crashed near Maidstone Road*
11th September	*– Churchill on radio. Warned German invasion near*

12th September – *Dozens of dog fights over Bobbing today. Another plane shot down. Three air raids*

13th September – *Four air raids today*

14th – 17th Sept – *25 air raids during this period*

18th September – *German dive bomber in sky towards Sheerness. Bus attacked by cannon shells from German plane near Kingsferry bridge. Junkers SS shot down*

19th September – *German plane shot down during air raid.*
Two air raids

20th September – *Two air raids today*

21st September – *Two air raids today*

22nd September – *Two air raids*

23rd September – *Saw one German plane come down and heard two others crash*

27th September – *Major German air raids all day. Over 100 planes shot down. Saw a number coming down*

28th September – *Watched parachute come down*

29th September – *Heard air-raid siren 'all clear', almost immediately followed by German bombers dropping bombs. Some fell on Sittingbourne High Street.*

As can be seen, not a day passed during this period without Bobbing residents having to take shelter from enemy aircraft, bombing and fighter attacks or without seeing or hearing airborne raids. For the school children at Bobbing School it was a period when they were constantly frightened by almost continuous waves of German fighters and bombers. Fortunately all were safe during this most intensive period of the War.

Charles Fairley's Battle of Britain diary continued on a detailed daily basis until the 17th November 1940 when he wrote '*Raids are now too frequent to keep detailed records or times. We now no longer take any notice of air raid warnings.*' After this time, he only recorded specific dates on which there were bombs falling, buildings destroyed, planes crashed in flames, major air raids or big dog fights.

During the four months of the Battle of Britain the Germans lost 1,733 aircraft, mainly over the Channel and southern England, while the British lost 1,379. By the end of 1940 the battle for supremacy in the skies over southern England had been won by the British RAF.

Later, towards the end of the War and with things going badly

Doodlebug flying rocket photographed over Bobbing in 1944

for Germany, they launched the first VI 'doodlebug' unmanned flying rocket attacks aimed at London and the south-east, using the A2 as a custom-built navigation route. Consequently, The A2 became known as 'Doodlebug Alley'. The missiles were engine driven with enough fuel to reach their target in the south-east or London. When the fuel ran out and the droning engine stopped the missile would drop to earth like a stone and explode, killing mostly innocent people. They were Adolf Hitler's way of using unmanned craft to bomb Britain.

The first of these weapons was fired at London on the 13th June 1944. In July of that year a VI rocket fell in Bobbing, fortunately in an orchard. Between then and the end of March, 1945, the Germans launched some 10,500 of these pilotless flying missiles at southern England, killing over 6,000 people and seriously injuring almost another 18,000. The last of these VIs was destroyed over Sittingbourne on March 27, 1945.

The VI was succeeded by the VII, a flying bomb propelled by rocket. Unlike the VI, these new rocket bombs travelled at speed and height and it was impossible to destroy them with gunfire like the earlier bombardment. In a period of just seven months in 1945, more than 1,000 of these flying bombs were fired at southern England, killing 2,754 people and injuring another 6,523.

Fortunately the Bobbing area came off relatively lightly during this intense period of World War II.

The story of the Bobbing oak

As part of the celebrations for Queen Victoria's Jubilee in 1887 the village of Bobbing decided to have a celebration party during which they would plant a commemorative oak tree at the top of Quinton Lane, where it joined Sheppey Way, and opposite Bobbing Place. Originally suggested by the landlord of Rose Hill House, Bobbing, the tree was planted on the day by Robert Taylor, who had been the gardener at Rose Hill House for some 47 years.

The festivities commenced with the grouping of all the school children from St. Bartholemew's School in the school yard for a photograph, after which they transferred to the church for the vicar to give a short service and all the children to sing 'God Save the Queen' heartily and reverently. Following this they walked to a meadow kindly lent for the day by Mr. Page of Bobbing Court.

At the Jubilee celebration there were said to be some 540 people (more than in the whole parish), including all the school children of Bobbing, who danced around the newly planted oak and were presented with Jubilee mugs to mark the occasion. Races of all kinds were held: two, three and four-legged races (wheelbarrow) for the children; races for young men and old men; races for maidens; races for ladies over 40. Unfortunately nobody entered for this category until the age was lowered to 30. Olive Stagg and Miss Lowe presented the prizes.

There were also cakes and lemonade, as well as a party in a nearby field with dancing to Mr. Brewer's Band. Games played included kiss in the ring, drop handerkerchief, skipping and tug of war. Tea of bread and butter and jam, biscuits and cake was set out on a table some 30 feet long and served by the Parish teachers, children served first, then adults.

Last, but no means least, there was an excellent display of fireworks which culminated in sending up of a huge fire balloon by Mr. Tomkins which, after a while, caught alight, to the immense delight of all the youngsters present who thought it was all part of the performance. The day was said to have been 'as enjoyable a treat as Bobbing had not seen for many years'.

Some 90 years later, in 1977, when planners were given a special brief for a £½ million road widening scheme for a half-mile section of the A249 Sittingbourne to Sheppey Road, they were given the message: 'Don't axe the Bobbing oak.' This followed protests from local people who were worried that the road widening might mean that the historic tree might be cut down.

However, once the County Council learned the significance of the Jubilee Oak Tree it was decided to integrate it into a new traffic island at the Quinton Road Junction where it was to stand in splendid isolation. This scheme did not materialize at the time although major road developments did take place around the Key Street crossroads. A new six-mile dual carriageway further to the south of the A249, known as the Iwade by-pass, was eventually built between the M2 Stockbury roundabout and Kingsferry Bridge as part of the new Bobbing plan launched in 1988.

The Bobbing Jubilee Oak therefore continued to proudly thrive, albeit battered by 20th century traffic along the Sheppey Way, on a small triangle of land, where the A249 Ferry Road branched off to Milton.

Unhappily, the Jubilee Oak was not to celebrate its first hundred years as it was crashed into by a large frozen food truck in January 1982 and severed at the roots.

However, despite being felled in this way, the oak continued to remain in the news. The Dolphin Barge Museum put in a bid to use the trunk and gracefully arched branches to restore the barge 'Ardeer.' Unfortunately this request was already too late. The old oak had already been hacked up into four-foot lengths and taken away to the council dump, thrown into a pit, and more than 50 tons of household rubbish pile onto it and then compacted in neat loads.

Drawing of the Bobbing Oak at the Sheppey Way and Milton junction by Peter Judges

A council spokesman said at the time: 'It is a case of being wise after the event. The request came too late and the immediate aim had been to clear the site; I doubt if its value as timber was assessed. It was a beautiful tree and a fine specimen but to have snapped so easily suggests that it may have been diseased at the base.'

Such was the ignominious end to the Bobbing Jubilee Oak which, it had been hoped in 1887, would have lasted for centuries. As part of the Bobbing plan it was proposed in 1998 that a replacement oak should be planted in the centre of a new roundabout at the junction. This never materialized as the council said the tree would be a traffic hazard.

However, Bobbing Women's Institute members had been able to plant another village tree in February 1983, albeit on the Sittingbourne side of the new Key Street roundabout, to commemorate the 1982 Royal wedding. The tree, a Norwegian maple, was donated by the council, while the W.I. raised money for a plaque to accompany the tree through a series of coffee mornings and cake sales.

Bobbing moves into the 21st Century

As Bobbing entered the 21st Century the changes that characterized much of the previous century and a half have continued – more demolition, more houses being built, more commercial property growing up, school expansion and other developments in and around the area.

Undoubtedly the predominant days of Bobbing's influence and power have long gone – the royal influence, the powerful barons and knights, the soldiers, the sheriffs and major land owners. So too, have many of the older buildings that made up much of the early history. There is little to show for the previous 2000 years of history that Bobbing can claim as its heritage. Nevertheless it is still important to catalogue some of this progress and ongoing change.

Opened to the first children in 1998, Demelza House Children's Hospice was built within a 6 acre site in rural Bobbing after four years of fund raising. Designed to look like a traditional Kentish farmhouse with the addition of a beautiful oast house in keeping with the Kent countryside, the Hospice was the inspiration of Derek and Jennifer Phillips, who set it up following the death of their daughter Demelza, from a brain tumour.

Today, in the 21st century, Demelza House, Bobbing, goes from strength to strength providing leadership and focus for many children, families and staff and also for supporters – and not just for very sick children. Any child with a life-limiting condition, fulfilling the criteria, at any stage of their illness or health, is welcomed. Countess Mountbatten of Burma is Patron of the charity.

Also coming to Bobbing as it entered the new century was a brand new pub-restaurant and hotel complex – called the Bobbing Apple Brewers Fayre which, together with a 40 bedroom Travel Inn were opened just off the A249 dual carriageway Sheppey Way at Bobbing Corner. A petrol station and shop are on the same site.

At about the same time, youngsters from Grove Park School were helping to plant trees and shrubs on ground for a new Meads Community Woodland. Members of the Countryside Working Group and the general public also attended. The scheme provides a woodland amenity area close to the housing developments that have grown up at Sonora Fields.

In a more sombre vein, work was scheduled to start in 2000 on a 30-acre plot north of Stickfast Lane, Bobbing, in a £1 million investment by the London Crematorium Company to build a new crematorium and green burial cemetery for the Sittingbourne area. The cemetery has enough land to last at least 20 years, parking for 45 cars and a chapel with 80 seats and up to 150 mourners, including standing room.

Although work on the crematorium was held up by a subsequent legal dispute over the land, building finally commenced in September 2002 and was opened in the summer of 2003. The completed complex has a wreath court, Book of Remembrance Room, gardens for scattering ashes and for memorial planting, a waiting area and administration section.

Ongoing concerns regarding the level of housing to be built on the Meads Estate between Bobbing and Milton Regis came to the fore again in February 2001, when permission was given for a further 200 houses on the Sonora Fields site. This was on top of the previous permission for 750 homes to built over a five year period. As part of the agreement with the developers it was agreed that they should also provide a new community hall and car park.

Plans were also approved for a scheme to knock down most of the old Keycol Hospital at Bobbing to make way for a Thames Gateway Trust plan to build 34 new homes, as well as for the health authority to repair and restore two former staff houses at the entrance to the development in Rook Lane.

In March 2001, residents of Bobbing were able to celebrate the arrival of a village sign on land opposite McDonalds, on the way into the village from Sheppey Way. The sign, which was made and designed by local antique dealer Tony Richards, had taken over a year to plan, make and erect.

The domed-topped sign, supported by two metal columns topped with acorns, shows the village church with a golden key – to represent the old Key Street Inn which, together with the post office, general store and mansion house, were at the busy centre of the village until they were demolished to make way for the A249 underpass. Also featured on the sign was an oak

The Bobbing Village sign. Drawing by Peter Judges.

tree. This represented the commemorative oak tree erected for Queen Victoria's Jubilee in 1887 which had stood at the junction of Quinton Lane and the old Sheppey Way until it was hit by a truck and severed at the roots in January 1982.

In 2001, a massive new extension to double the size of Bobbing Village School to 220 pupils was approved by Kent planners. This major extension has now been completed.

On a smaller scale a Bobbing pub, the Halfway House, underwent a complete external facelift at the end of 2002, together with being given a new name – The Dancing Dog Saloon. The pub became the headquarters for the owners' North and South Line Dancing Team, which had 400 members from the Sheppey and Medway areas.

Such have been the ongoing changes to the way of life in Bobbing. Perhaps insignificant when compared with what has happened over the previous two thousand years or so, it is nevertheless important to continue to catalogue change and evolution so that those that follow in the years to come can have a sense of the history and heritage of what this small community has been able to offer to the County of Kent, to England and, in some cases, to the wider world.

Acknowledgements

Much of the early research for this book was undertaken by Dorothy Fairley, a resident of Bobbing, during the 1950s, 1960s and into the 1990s. This has more recently been continued by Michael Fairley, her son, and additional material has been provided through research, pictures and drawings compiled over many years by Peter Judges. Thanks are due to all of these for the more than 50 years of work that has gone into preparing the final version of this book on Bobbing.

Thanks are also due to Peter Morgan and the Sittingbourne Heritage Museum for additional material, photography and for the Preface to the book.

Acknowledgement is also made to the many sources of reference and study that were used in researching this history of Bobbing and in particular to:

Archaelogicia Cantiana records

Bobbing Tithe award schedule

Bobbing Village Design Statement

'Borden – The history of a Kentish Parish' by Helen Allinson

Canterbury Cathedral Archives

Centre for Kentish Studies

East Kent Gazette

Here's History Kent

'Historic Churches' website

Kent Archives

Kent County Council: Kent Parish Councils records

Maidstone Museum

Medway City Archives

'Memories of Key Street' by Peter Judges

Mr Batt, for his collection of memorabilia and other articles

Sittingbourne Heritage Museum

'The Founding of Maryland' website

The Kent Family History Society

'The Turnpike Roads of Kent' by James Carley